PSYCHOANALYTIC CONCEPTS AND THE STRUCTURAL THEORY

Journal of the American Psychoanalytic Association
Monograph Series Number Three

PSYCHOANALYTIC CONCEPTS AND THE STRUCTURAL THEORY

JACOB A. ARLOW
and
CHARLES BRENNER

International Universities Press, Inc.

NEW YORK   **NEW YORK**

Contents

Foreword

THIS, the third monograph sponsored by the Journal of the American Psychoanalytic Association, expresses the continued interest, already evident in previous monographs, that many analysts have shown in elaborations of psychoanalytic ego psychology. This particular work represents a systematic synthesis of Arlow's and Brenner's thinking on this subject, some of which has been expressed in previous contributions. They seek to demonstrate that there is essentially little in the topographic model of the psyche which cannot be more satisfactorily explained by the structural model.

To some extent the authors elaborate upon Freud's own dissatisfaction with certain aspects of the topographic model, considerations which ultimately led him to the formulation of the structural model. In Freud's prolific writing he often neglected to make a retrospective reformulation when new contributions proved to be incompatible with former theories. The authors attempt to clarify and resolve such contradictions, particularly in the papers on metapsychology. This has been a considerable effort and will be appreciated by many who have been confused by the apparent inconsistencies in some of Freud's formulations.

An appreciation of the comprehensiveness of the authors' analysis of the problem can be achieved by taking account of the many areas they survey in comparing the two models. Among the basic theoretical concepts reviewed are those of the preconscious and the unconscious, primary and secondary processes, regression, and the psychoanalytic psychology of dreams and psychosis.

In so far as their purpose is that of clarification and the resolution of inconsistencies Arlow and Brenner will find many in agreement. But they go beyond this by suggesting the abandonment of many concepts inherent in the topographic model. Expressing their views in the clear and coherent style so characteristic of them, the authors certainly leave no room for any misunderstanding of their unequivocal statement that, since the topographic and structural models of the mind are incompatible with each other, the former should be discarded. They treat the models as forthright dichotomies and, in detailing the inconsistencies between them, have no trouble in deciding in favor of the structural model. They do not feel that much is to be gained by an attempt to integrate the two.

We anticipate a variety of reactions to this monograph. Some may applaud the authors' efforts as a valuable and much-needed contribution to psychoanalytic theory. Others may feel that there is much in the topographic model which is useful in application to clinical phenomena, and that its abandonment would leave a void not completely filled by the structural model. Such analysts are of the opinion that Freud intended to find a place within the structural model for many of the features of the topographic one which are of clinical as well as theoretical value. There are some who may even believe that the structural model, in paving the

way toward a psychoanalytic ego psychology, will itself ultimately have to be superseded.

The editors of the Journal feel that it is the publication
of just such controversial subject matter which may constitute one of the functions of a monograph. It is our own
expectation that this provocative monograph will stimulate
further study as well as discussions for some time to come.

THE EDITORS

Preface

THIS MONOGRAPH represents a summary of many years of joint thought and effort. During these years we have attempted to clarify our own understanding of the ever-expanding body of psychoanalytic theory. Our aim was to correlate this theory in a consistent fashion with clinical data and with our therapeutic work. We have tried to understand the fundamental concepts of psychoanalysis from the broadest point of view.

We are fully aware that psychoanalysis as a science will continue to develop in many directions. We anticipate that, as in the case of all sciences, important concepts may undergo revision and transformation and that some of them may lose their position of commanding significance. This has been true of psychoanalysis in the past and will undoubtedly be true in the future. Accordingly, the views which we present in this monograph, we do not consider to be fixed, permanent, complete, official, or dogmatic. They represent our understanding of the relationship among the fundamental concepts of psychoanalysis at the present stage of its development.

Our main line of reasoning takes its origin, quite naturally, in the later writings of Freud. In addition we have been influenced especially, as has our entire generation of psychoanalysts, by the work of A. Freud, O. Fenichel, H. Hartmann,

E. Kris, and R. M. Loewenstein. Our indebtedness is well documented in the many references to them in the monograph. We owe special thanks to our close friends and colleagues of the past two decades, Dr. David Beres and Dr. Martin Wangh. When the present work was first projected we had hoped that the four of us would be co-authors. Such a collaboration would have been a most natural one. Many of the ideas here expressed have their origins in the frequent meetings and discussions which we four have enjoyed for so many years. However, other interests and commitments of our colleagues precluded their sharing the task of authorship with us. With their usual generosity, they have read and discussed with us nearly every paragraph we have written. We are immeasurably indebted to our two friends for many valuable ideas, though we as authors necessarily bear responsibility for what this book contains.

To many readers various chapters of this monograph may sound familiar. This is due to the fact that during the past eight years sections of this monograph have been read before psychoanalytic meetings[1] in different parts of the United States as well as at the International Psycho-Analytical Congresses. We have benefited greatly from the discussions which followed these presentations. In the process of revision and rewriting, we have taken advantage of the criticisms and suggestions given by our colleagues. In a certain sense, therefore, we are indebted to many of our colleagues for this final version of the monograph.

JACOB A. ARLOW, M.D.
CHARLES BRENNER, M.D.

New York, July 1963

[1] Chapters 6 and 8 were presented in the years 1958-1960; Chapters 7, 9, and 10, in the years 1960-1963. Chapters 1 to 5 were included, in abbreviated form, as introductory material in most of the above presentations.

[xii]

PSYCHOANALYTIC CONCEPTS AND THE STRUCTURAL THEORY

1

Introduction

THIS BOOK HAS been in the writing for the past six years. It grew out of the impression that there are several areas of psychoanalytic theory and practice which are victims of what might be called a cultural lag. In those areas analysts by and large have not yet taken full advantage of the opportunities for progress which the structural theory has to offer. In addition, there is still evidence of a failure to recognize clearly that there are basically important differences between the structural theory of the mind, which Freud first clearly outlined in 1923 in *The Ego and the Id,* and his earlier theory, which dates from 1900 and is called the topographic theory.

These facts are the more surprising because of the important place which the structural theory already occupies in psychoanalytic thinking. It is generally recognized by analysts that the introduction of the structural theory by Freud was both a theoretical innovation of the first order and the basis for a major advance in technique as well. The whole of what we call ego analysis today was made possible by the introduction of the structural theory in 1923 and of its corollary, the current theory of anxiety, in 1926. It is these theories that have made possible the consistent analysis of the ego's defenses and the therapeutic approach to character neuroses, which so clearly differentiate modern psychoanalytic technique from what went before. It is an exceptional event when an analyst (Kubie, 1958) decries the use of the concepts ego, id, and superego and turns back to the concepts of the topographic theory for his formulation of the psychopathology of the neuroses and of the conflicts of the normal mind. The structural theory is firmly entrenched in psychoanalytic thinking today and is considered to be an essential part of its theoretical framework by nearly every analyst.

To emphasize the fruitfulness and value of the structural theory may consequently seem to be belaboring the obvious. Nevertheless, despite the nearly universal acceptance accorded the structural theory among psychoanalysts, it appears that the full nature and extent of its implications for psychoanalytic theory and practice have not been generally appreciated.

Hartmann, Kris, and Loewenstein made this point many years ago (1946; see also Hartmann, 1950b, 1958; Kris, 1950b). Their own subsequent writings, collaborative as well as individual, have done much to remedy the lack of full understanding of the place of the structural theory in psychoanalysis, nor have they been alone in performing this valuable service. As an outstanding example one might mention Fenichel's *Psychoanalytic Theory of Neurosis* (1945). Yet it appears that much still remains to be done along these lines.

For example, it seems fair to say that many, probably most psychoanalysts today consider the structural theory and the topographic theory to be equally valid. The idea seems to be that each explains certain facts better than the other and that each, therefore, is valid in its own sphere. Thus both theories, most analysts maintain, can be used side by side without interfering with each other. This view, widely expressed or implied in oral discussion among analysts, has less often appeared in psychoanalytic writings. It may be found occasionally in the literature in explicit form, however, as in the following quotation from Lewin (1952). In a discussion of the different terms of the topographic and the structural theories Lewin wrote, "Nowadays most writers use both terminologies, the older when discussing dreams, the newer when writing about the neuroses. This cleavage is not deep-seated. It is due in the main to convenience and tradition, just as in mathematics certain formulations (the algebraic, geometric, trigonometric, etc.) are more convenient and more wieldy for one or another problem. Ordinarily such considerations offset any disadvantages arising from a double terminology" (p. 295f.).

An opinion so reasonable, so widely accepted, and so well expressed by so eminent an authority necessarily carries great weight. Nonetheless, it is our conviction that the topographic and the structural theories are neither compatible nor interchangeable.[1] We maintain that it is actually disadvantageous to use the terms of the two theories interchangeably and to speak of the id, the ego, and the superego in one breath and of the unconscious, the preconscious, and the conscious in the next, a practice which, as Lewin correctly observes, is so widespread among analysts as to be nearly universal.

The two theories, in fact, which are so similar in many respects, are so different in others as to be incompatible with one another. Nor are these differences of minor importance. On the contrary, they have principally to do with the topic of unconscious mental conflict, an area of vital importance in psychoanalysis.

In the chapters which follow we shall endeavor to demonstrate the correctness of the view just expressed. We shall also attempt to show that where the two theories do differ from each other, the structural theory is the more satisfactory of

---

[1] Since the above was written, Gill (1963) has also pointed to the fact that the structural theory differs from the topographic one in basic ways.

the two. It is distinctly superior to the topographic one. For this reason it has largely replaced the topographic theory, often to a greater degree than has been explicitly realized. It is, we feel, the theory which psychoanalysts should apply to the understanding of all mental phenomena.

We also propose to explore some of the implications of the structural theory other than its incompatibility with the topographic theory. That is, we shall also attempt to discuss certain changes which, though required by the structural theory, have not yet been made in theoretical concepts and formulations which originated at a time before the introduction of the structural theory. These concepts have, as it were, been held over from the topographic theory. Compatible though they are with that theory, and valuable as they have been to us in the past, these concepts are in need of substantial revision if they are to be thoroughly coherent with our current conceptual framework and to be of maximum use to us at present.

The relation between the theory of psychoanalysis and its practice is a particularly close one. This statement is familiar to every psychoanalyst from frequent repetition. We shall attempt to illustrate it at every opportunity in the chapters to follow and particularly in the chapters on dreams and on psychoses, respectively. It is precisely because the structural theory led to a revolutionary improvement in psychoanalytic practice that it is of such great importance. The more consistently one applies the concepts of the structural theory and the more thoroughly one exploits them, the greater the advantage to one's clinical understanding and technique.

It may be worth while to make a few general remarks at this point about the two theories which we shall discuss at such length as well as about their relation to psychoanalytic theory as a whole.

[4]

Freud very early introduced the concept of a mental or psychic apparatus, whose function it is to deal with the energies of the mind by binding or discharging them. The first systematic statement[2] of such a concept appeared in 1900 in Chapter VII of *The Interpretation of Dreams*. Freud subsequently made various emendations of the ideas contained in that chapter concerning the psychic apparatus, but its basic elements remained unchanged for many years. In the metapsychological papers of 1915 as in Chapter VII, the psychic apparatus was conceived of as comprising three systems, called the Unconscious (*Ucs.*), the Preconscious (*Pcs.*), and the Conscious (*Cs.*) or Perceptual-Conscious (*Pcpt.-Cs.*) respectively, of which the systems *Pcs.* and *Cs.* were sometimes grouped together as the system *Cs.-Pcs.* because of the intimate functional relationship between them. The three systems, *Ucs., Pcs.,* and *Cs.,* were often referred to as regions of the mind, and it is for this reason that the theory of the psychic apparatus which includes them is generally known as the topographic one.

In 1923, in *The Ego and the Id,* Freud introduced major conceptual changes and a new terminology into the psychoanalytic theory of the psychic apparatus, for reasons which we shall discuss in detail in Chapter 3. He discarded the idea of dividing the psychic apparatus according to the accessibility or inaccessibility of its various elements to consciousness. Instead he proposed to distinguish two systems within the mind which he called the id and the ego. The ego was further subdivided by distinguishing within it a particular group of mutually related functions to be called the superego. Because

2 The Project (1895a) may be regarded as Freud's first attempt to conceptualize a psychic apparatus. He decided, however, not to publish it and was opposed to its publication when Marie Bonaparte discovered this historic document among the Fliess letters (Kris, 1950c).

these innovations were of a major order, their introduction is usually signalized by calling Freud's second theory of the psychic apparatus by a new name: the structural theory.

It is customary, therefore, to distinguish between two psychoanalytic theories of the psychic apparatus of which the one, the topographic theory, divides the apparatus into systems on the basis of the criterion: accessible to consciousness vs. inaccessible to consciousness, while the other, the structural theory, divides it on the basis: inner world (manifestations of the instinctual drives) vs. outer world (external environment).

It is important to realize that the distinction between these two theories and the nomenclature which marks that distinction are essentially matters of generally accepted custom and convenience. The structural and topographic theories were never named as such and presented by Freud in finished or "final" form. They are groups of related ideas within the area of psychoanalytic theory which have never been precisely delineated. That is, no one has ever said explicitly which parts of psychoanalytic theory prior to 1923 were to be included within the term "topographic theory" nor which parts after 1923 were to be understood as comprising the structural theory. It has simply been understood in a general way that each theory comprises a group of related ideas having to do particularly with the nature and functioning of what Freud called the mental apparatus.

Another important point to bear in mind during the discussion which follows is the relationship between the topographic and the structural theories on the one hand and the theory of the instinctual drives on the other. In essence these two parts of psychoanalytic theory are inseparable. They are two aspects of a single whole. Freud (1900, 1915b) conceived of the psychic apparatus as an agency for the regulation and

[6]

discharge of mental energy; the source of that energy was identified as the instinctual drives (Freud, 1905). The drives, as their name implies, drive or impel the mind to activity. They generate what Freud called mental energy, using the analogy of the physical concept of energy as the quantitative measure of the capacity to do work. As we shall see, the psychic apparatus is described very largely in terms of how it deals with mental energy. Moreover, as we shall also see, the introduction of the current classification of the instinctual drives into libidinal and aggressive ones (Freud, 1920) seems to be significantly related to the introduction of the structural theory shortly thereafter (Freud, 1923a; Hartmann, 1948). It is thus impossible to discuss the topographic and the structural theories of the mental apparatus without frequent reference to the instinctual drives, and in particular to mental energies which derive from the drives. However, we shall not attempt any detailed discussion of the origin of the instinctual drives, of their nature, or of their classification. Such a detailed discussion is not essential for the purpose of our present work.

Another observation of general significance to psychoanalytic theory may likewise be in place here. Psychoanalysis takes for granted two basic assumptions. One of these is that mental processes are no more chance, arbitrary, or disconnected than are physical ones. On the contrary, they follow the same general laws of cause and effect which we customarily assume to operate in the physical world. Psychoanalysis postulates that psychic determinism is as strict as physical determinism. It is true that psychic causes or determinants are nearly always complex and multiple, whereas physical determinants are often few and simple by comparison. However, this difference in degree does not imply any difference in principle.[3] The second assumption is that many mental processes, including some of the most important determinants of behavior and of conscious thought, go on in the mind quite without conscious awareness. In other words, "conscious" and "mental" are by no means synonymous. This second axiom of psychoanalytic theory has become so widely accepted that few readers of the present work are likely even to consider the possibility of its being challenged. The facts in its favor, largely facts deriving from the application of the psychoanalytic method, are by now overwhelming. It is hard to realize that in 1915 the situation was so different that Freud considered it necessary to devote the entire opening section of "The Unconscious" to a discussion of the merits of this basic assumption.

We have mentioned these two basic assumptions of psychoanalytic theory as a reminder to the reader that these assumptions underlie both the topographic theory and the structural theory. For a fuller discussion of the two assumptions readers are referred to Brenner (1955a).

With these various considerations in mind we may now proceed to the task of carrying out the aims we have set ourselves in this monograph. The chapter to follow will contain the first step in this task, which is an exposition of the principal features of the first of Freud's theories of the mental apparatus, namely the topographic theory.

[3] For an extended discussion of this subject, published since the above was written, see Waelder (1963).

2

The Topographic Theory

THE TOPOGRAPHIC THEORY was first presented in Chapter VII of *The Interpretation of Dreams* (1900). This chapter and "The Unconscious" (1915b) will be the principal sources of reference for the outline to follow.

Freud decided to formulate the topographic theory as a general theory of how the apparatus of the mind functions because he had discovered that the psychology of neurotic symptom formation is essentially the same as that of certain aspects of normal mental functioning, namely, dreams, jokes, and parapraxes. By using the technique of psychoanalysis, Freud was able to discover identical, unconscious mental processes at work in the minds of the neurotic, the dreamer, and the normal, waking adult. We emphasize this fact because it is often erroneously assumed that the topographic theory derives principally or wholly from the study of dreams, since it was first expounded in *The Interpretation of Dreams*. The fact is that Freud himself (1900, pp. 588, 597ff.) explicitly stated that this was not the case, and that it was his earlier work on the psychology of the neuroses that laid the groundwork for his understanding of the psychology of the dream. What impressed Freud as being of particular importance was that the psychological differences between the neurotic and the normal are quantitative differences rather than qualitative ones; they are differences of degree, not differences of kind.

If one bears in mind the importance of the role which Freud's understanding of the neuroses played in the formulation of the topographic theory, one can understand better certain aspects of the theory itself. His experience in treating the neuroses by the technique of psychoanalysis had convinced him that the crucially important factor in neurotic symptom formation has to do with whether or not certain mental elements are accessible to consciousness. The mental elements in question, he had discovered, are wishes for pleasurable gratification which are in conflict with the patient's moral standards and mature goals. Freud's experience convinced him that if the wishes which give rise to such an intrapsychic conflict are inaccessible to consciousness (repressed), they may, if they become strong enough, give rise to a neurotic symptom. If, on the other hand, a repressed wish can be made conscious by psychoanalytic treatment, the symptom to which it has given rise will disappear. It is only when a wish is unconscious, he concluded, that it can be pathogenic.

It was in accordance with these insights that Freud proposed in the topographic theory to divide the mental apparatus as he did. According to the theory, there are to be three systems of the mind, each of which is characterized essentially by its relationship to consciousness. The system *Ucs.* comprises those mental elements which are accessible to consciousness only with difficulty or not at all. The system *Pcs.* comprises those mental elements which are readily accessible to consciousness. Finally, the system *Cs.* includes whatever is conscious at any given moment. Between the systems *Ucs.* and *Pcs.* there operates an intersystemic censor which enables the system *Pcs.* to exclude objectionable elements of the system *Ucs.* and to refuse them entry, figuratively speaking, into the system *Cs.* As we shall see, there is much more than this that the topographic theory has to say about each of the three systems which it postulates. We wish to emphasize the following: that the central idea of the topographic theory is that the psychic apparatus can be divided into systems on the basis of their relationship to consciousness. As regards mental conflict, what is of prime importance in the topographic theory is whether the wish which gives rise to conflict is or is not accessible to consciousness. Freud (1915b) himself made this clear. In "The Unconscious" (p. 172) he mentioned the possibility of an alternative basis for dividing the mental apparatus and rejected it because, he said, whether a particular mental element is conscious or not is the starting point of our investigations as analysts. He maintained that we must therefore hold to it as a guide to our theoretical formulations. It is worth noting, parenthetically, that the alternative basis which Freud rejected in 1915 was precisely the one which he eventually adopted in 1923 as the central idea of the structural theory. We can see here clearly one of the basic differences between the topographic and the structural theory, a topic which we shall discuss at length in a later chapter.

Having established (1) that the topographic theory largely reflects Freud's experience in analyzing neurotic patients, and (2) that in accordance with that experience it depicts the mind in general as divided into separate systems on the basis of accessibility to consciousness, we may proceed to present the topographic theory in more detail.

Just a few words of definition. (1) The amount of mental energy invested in a mental process or representation is called its cathexis. (2) The aspect of mental functioning which has to do with the amount of mental energy involved in any particular mental phenomenon is called the economic (i.e., quantitative) aspect of that phenomenon. (3) We have already defined mental energy itself as deriving from the instinctual drives and as impelling the mind to activity. It is assumed that instinctual gratification results in a discharge of mental energy and that mental activity of whatever sort is accompanied by a transfer or flow of mental energy.

We propose now to discuss in some detail each of the three mental systems which are postulated by the topographic theory.

THE SYSTEM *Ucs.*

As already noted, the system *Ucs.* is defined by the fact that its elements are (1) inaccessible to consciousness. In addition it is characterized (2) by a particular mode of functioning, known as the primary process; (3) by the nonverbal nature of its memory traces; (4) by the fact that it is incapable of any form of mentation other than to wish, i.e., by the fact that it operates according to the pleasure principle; (5) by its relation to the instinctual life; and (6) by its generally infantile character.

1. *Inaccessibility to Consciousness.* The normal route of access to consciousness from the system *Ucs.* lies through the system *Pcs.* The unconscious element must first become preconscious before it can become conscious. What this implies will be discussed more fully in the section on the system *Pcs.* Certain elements of the system *Ucs.* are excluded from the system *Pcs.* by the action of the intersystemic censor. The action of this censor is called repression. Those elements of the system *Ucs.* which are denied access to the system *Pcs.* by repression are called collectively the repressed part of the system *Ucs.*, or more often simply "the repressed." There are

ways in which elements of the system *Ucs.* may gain access to consciousness other than the normal one just described.

(a) Symptoms. If the censor is enfeebled or if the repressed becomes too strong, elements from the repressed overpower the censor and force their way into consciousness despite its opposition. Such a failure of repression results in neurotic or psychotic symptoms. In other words, the censor is the guardian of mental health. In so far as it is successful in controlling the repressed and in excluding it from access to consciousness we are mentally healthy. If it fails in this function and must compromise with the repressed or even succumb to it altogether, we are mentally ill.

(b) Wit and jokes. An element of the repressed may gain access to consciousness in special ways and under special circumstances without compromising the individual's mental health. Examples of this may be seen in wit and humor, as the following quotation (Freud, 1915a) makes clear: "Special techniques have been evolved, with the purpose of bringing about such changes in the play of mental forces that what would otherwise give rise to unpleasure may on this occasion result in pleasure; and, whenever a technical device of this sort comes into operation, the repression of an instinctual representative which would otherwise be repudiated is removed. These techniques have till now only been studied in any detail in jokes. As a rule the repression is only temporarily removed and is promptly reinstated" (p. 151).

(c) Dreaming. During sleep otherwise repressed elements from the system *Ucs.* gain access to consciousness as dreams. In part this is due to a relaxation of the censor during sleep. In part, however, it is due to the fact that energies of the system *Ucs.* are able during sleep to traverse the mental apparatus in a reverse direction and to cathect visual memory

[13]

traces with sufficient intensity to cause them to become conscious as sense perceptions, i.e., as images of a dream. If the same regressive flow of energy with the same result occurs during waking life, the result is a pathological one, i.e., a hallucination. Such a hallucination is assumed to occur normally in very early life, however. It is then referred to as a hallucinatory wish fulfillment.

2. *Primary Process.* Thus far we have discussed the relationship between the systems *Ucs.* and *Pcs.* in spatial terms, as though each were a region of the mind which could be physically and spatially distinguished from the other. This is a convenient fiction for many purposes. Indeed it is responsible for the very name of the theory, since "topographic" means "having to do with the configuration of an area." However, even in 1900 Freud made it clear that the systems of the mind he proposed to distinguish cannot be thought of as different localities except in a figurative sense, and he repeated this in "The Unconscious" in 1915. He explained that the proper way to define the systems *Ucs.* and *Pcs.* is in terms of energy discharge and potential. The system *Ucs.*, for example, is properly defined as comprising those mental elements and processes which function according to the primary process. The systems *Pcs.* and *Cs.* by the same token comprise whatever in the mind functions according to the secondary process. Since we are at the moment concerned with a description of the system *Ucs.*, the question for us to answer here is: "What is the primary process?"

The primary process is so called because it is the earlier of the two modes of mental functioning which are distinguished by the topographic theory. In early childhood, when the system *Ucs.* comprises nearly the whole of the mental apparatus, its mode of operation is the only mode of functioning of the mind. Not until later does a different mode of functioning, to be called the secondary process, appear. The words "primary" and "secondary" have only this temporal, developmental connotation. They are not intended to convey any idea of relative importance. In fact, the secondary process is assumed to become dominant eventually in the normal adult.

The principal feature of the primary process is a tendency to the complete discharge of mental energies without delay. Thus cathexes of mental energy subject to the primary process press continuously for discharge. This may be observed, for example, in connection with the instinctual wishes of early childhood, when the primary process holds undisputed sway over the mind. It is easy to see how imperiously such wishes demand gratification. The same imperious demand for gratification characterizes instinctual demands within the system *Ucs.* throughout life.

Two other characteristics of the primary process are (a) that cathexes of mental energy which follow the primary process are readily displaced, or highly mobile, and (b) that such cathexes are readily condensed. The clinical observations which lend support to these assumptions are the following. When one is able to trace back to their origins the consequences of the operation of the primary process, i.e., when one is able to analyze a neurotic symptom, a dream, a joke, or a parapraxis, one often discovers that in the course of formation of the symptom, dream, etc., ideas and images have substituted one for the other with an ease and freedom quite different from what one is used to in ordinary, conscious thinking. Such observations are accounted for by the concept of ready displaceability of cathexes. Cathexes pass easily from one idea or image to another. They are highly mobile. In addition, one discovers from such analyses that many ideas are often represented by a single thought or image. That is,

[15]

the cathexes originally distributed over many mental elements have become condensed on a single element.

3. *Nonverbal Nature of Memory Traces.* Memory traces, i.e., mental residua of sensory perceptions, are assumed to be of various sorts and variously grouped within the mind (Freud, 1900, p. 538). A particularly important distinction is to be made between those memory traces which are nonverbal in nature and those which are verbal. A nonverbal memory trace might consist, for example, of the memory of the visual image of a face, or of a scene, or of any other sensory percept which was perceived at a time of life before there were words to describe or name the percept in question. A verbal memory trace would be one in which the remembered object or scene was named or thought of in words at the same time it was perceived sensorily. If this were all, the distinction would be a simple one. It would be merely a distinction between memories dating from the preverbal (prelanguage) period of life and those of the time of life after the acquisition of language. However, there is much more than this to the distinction between verbal and nonverbal memory traces in the topographic theory. According to the topographic theory, memory traces can be *changed* from nonverbal to verbal or from verbal to nonverbal. These changes result from cathectic shifts within the mind and when they occur they represent a change from the system *Ucs.* to the system *Pcs.* or vice versa. The idea is this. A nonverbal memory belongs by definition to the system *Ucs.* If a nonverbal memory joins with the memory trace of the corresponding word(s), the cathexes of the two are combined so that the resultant verbal memory trace has a larger cathexis than the original nonverbal memory trace had. It is said to be hypercathected. It then, again by definition, belongs to the system *Pcs.* In other words, for a memory trace of the system *Ucs.*

[16]

to become preconscious it must increase its cathexis by joining with the corresponding word trace(s). If the reverse happens, and a memory trace of the system *Pcs.* is broken up into its two component parts, the nonverbal memory trace of lower cathexis which is one of the parts then becomes part of the system *Ucs.* and is repressed. That is, repression is describable as a withdrawal of cathexis, specifically as a withdrawal of the word cathexis. Thus memory traces of the system *Ucs.*, whether repressed or not, are nonverbal.

The reason for this painstaking distinction between verbal and nonverbal memory traces as well as for their careful separation into the two systems *Pcs.* and *Ucs.* is very simple and eminently clinical. Freud had found repressed wishes and forgotten memories to underlie every neurotic symptom. When these could gain access to consciousness, when they could be verbalized in the analytic situation, the symptom disappeared. It was in correspondence with these clinical findings that he was led to assume that memory traces of the system Ucs. are nonverbal while those of the system *Pcs.* are verbal.

4. *Wish Fulfillment.* From his study of dreams as well as of neurotic symptoms Freud (1900) came to the realization that the motive force supplied to either dream or symptom from the system *Ucs.* is describable as a desire for the fulfillment of a wish. As he stated in another connection (Freud, 1911a), the system *Ucs.* operates according to the pleasure principle.

5. *Relation to the Instinctual Life.* In 1905 Freud published the first statement of his theory of instincts. Though he divided the instincts into two broad groups, the ego instincts and the sexual instincts, it was the latter to which he devoted his principal attention, since it was about them that he had made such brilliant and such astonishing discoveries with the help of the psychoanalytic method. Of these discov-

eries the chief one, it will be remembered, was the proper appreciation of the importance of infantile sexuality. Once the theory of the sexual drives had been established, these drives were recognized as the source of the motive force or mental energy belonging to the system *Ucs.* In other words, according to the topographic theory, (a) the elements of the system *Ucs.* are the mental representatives and derivatives of the sexual drives, and (b) the mental energy associated with these derivatives is sexual mental energy, or libido. The activity of the system *Ucs.* results from libidinal tensions, i.e., it is directed toward the satisfaction of the individual's sexual wishes.

6. *Infantile Nature.* The generally infantile nature of the system *Ucs.* is related to several of its characteristics which we have already listed. First, it is the first or primary part of the mental apparatus. The systems *Pcs.* and *Cs.,* it will be remembered, develop only later. Thus the system *Ucs.* operates throughout life in the same way as the entire mind operates during infancy, namely, according to the primary process. Like the little child, the system *Ucs.* wants its wishes gratified without delay; it is interested only in gratification, i.e., in libidinal discharge. Second, mentation in the system *Ucs.* tends to be nonverbal, as it is in infancy. Such language function as there is, is visual and primitive at best. Third, like those of the child, the libidinal demands of the system *Ucs.* follow the pleasure principle. They take little heed of external reality. The reality principle, as Freud (1911a) named it, develops *pari passu* with the system *Pcs.* It is a regulatory principle of the systems *Pcs.* and *Cs.,* not of the system *Ucs.* Fourth, an important part of the system *Ucs.* consists of the fantasies and experiences of childhood and adolescence (Freud, 1908) which have been repressed by the system *Pcs.* in the course of its development because those experiences

[18]

and fantasies are the mental representatives of infantile sexual wishes which are unacceptable to the system *Pcs.* Thus an important part of the system *Ucs.* is infantile in the sense that the experiences, fantasies, and wishes of childhood live on in it unchanged, though repudiated (repressed) by the more adult part of the mind.

THE SYSTEM *Pcs.*

1. The system *Pcs.* comprises those elements of the mind which are accessible to consciousness. For an element of the system *Ucs.* to become conscious, it must first become preconscious. This it does, as we have already seen, by becoming joined to the corresponding word traces. Thus elements of the system *Pcs.*, and in particular memory traces which belong to that system, are verbal in nature.

2. The censor between the systems *Ucs.* and *Pcs.* is a part of or one of the functions of the latter system. If the censor withdraws the word cathexis from a memory trace of the system *Pcs.*, that memory trace is repressed and is thenceforth part of the system *Ucs.* If the censor withholds cathexis from an element of the system *Ucs.*, that element must remain part of the system *Ucs.* It is likewise repressed. If, on the other hand, the censor permits an element of the system *Ucs.* to be cathected by the energy of the corresponding word memory, that element becomes a part of the system *Pcs.* and is thus accessible to consciousness.

3. The system *Pcs.* is not present from birth. It begins to develop in childhood, and as the individual grows to adulthood the system *Pcs.* gradually achieves ascendancy in the functioning of the mind. Because it is a secondary development in mental life, the mode of functioning which is characteristic of the system *Pcs.* is called the secondary process. The

principal difference between the secondary and the primary processes is this. Mental energy which follows the primary process presses for immediate discharge, i.e., wishes of the system *Ucs.* strive for immediate gratification. On the other hand, mental energy which follows the secondary process can be bound, i.e., its discharge can be delayed temporarily or even, perhaps, indefinitely. In other words, wishes of instinctual origin which have gained access to the system *Pcs.* still press for gratification, but gratification may be postponed for a longer or shorter time in accordance with external realities, with the individual's own moral standards, etc. The system *Ucs.*, like the infant, is interested only in immediate gratification. The system *Pcs.*, a product of adulthood, is realistic, willing to wait, able to control its instinctual wishes.

4. The influence of realistic considerations upon the functioning of the system *Pcs.* is formulated as a regulatory principle of the mind, called the reality principle. The system *Ucs.* operates solely according to what is called the pleasure-unpleasure principle, or, more simply, the pleasure principle. According to this principle, the system *Ucs.* operates solely to avoid unpleasure and to achieve pleasure. It will be noted that this is identical with the earlier statement that in the system *Ucs.* instinctual energy seeks prompt and complete discharge. The system *Pcs.*, on the other hand, though it too follows the pleasure principle, does so only with modifications. It delays the pleasurable discharge of instinctual energy in accordance with the dictates of reality, of conscience, of logic, etc. Thus the capacity to bind cathexes is intimately connected with the functioning of the reality principle, just as mobility of cathexes subserves the pleasure principle.

5. The binding of mental energy and the consequent delay in its discharge which characterize the functioning of the system *Pcs.* results in a higher cathectic level within the

system *Pcs.* as a whole than exists in the system *Ucs.* in which mental energy is discharged as quickly as possible. Mental energy builds up within the system *Pcs.* much as water will be stored up behind a dam that prevents it from flowing away freely and promptly. The fact that the system *Pcs.* has such stored-up mental energy available to it permits it to function in a more precise and discriminating way than can the system *Ucs.* In particular, it can engage in that type of trial action that we call thought. In doing so it can solve problems without the great expenditure of mental energy that would be required by full action on a trial-and-error basis. It can accomplish the same result by expending a relatively very small amount of mental energy in thinking. Thus the functioning of the system *Pcs.* is more precise, more discriminating, and expends less mental energy than does the functioning of the system *Ucs.*

THE SYSTEM *Cs.*

We have already noted the close relationship between the system *Cs.* and the system *Pcs.* This is a relationship that develops *pari passu* with the development of the system *Pcs.* The tendency is for conscious awareness to be limited to (1) sensations due to stimuli from the outer world, and (2) events, i.e., thoughts, memories, emotions, etc., within the system *Pcs.* In other words, the normal waking adult is not directly conscious of anything going on in the system *Ucs.* As far as what is going on within his own mind is concerned, he can be conscious only of what is going on in the system *Pcs.* Elements of that system can be made conscious by being cathected by the system *Cs.* This cathexis is called the cathexis of attention. Elements of the system *Ucs.* cannot ordinarily be cathected by the system *Cs.*, that is, they cannot attract or receive the cathexis of attention. They must first become preconscious by being joined with the corresponding word trace. Thus, for an element of the system *Ucs.* to become conscious it must receive an additional cathexis or hypercathexis from two sources. First it must be cathected by the system *Pcs.*, i.e., it must receive the word cathexis that belongs to it; and second it must receive attention cathexis from the system *Cs.* Exceptions to this rule are to be found in dreaming, in jokes, and above all in neurotic symptom formation. Thus, for example, an obsessional idea does not become conscious by first being cathected by the system *Pcs.* On the contrary, it becomes conscious despite every effort on the part of the censor of the system *Pcs.* to repress it.

The system *Cs.*, in addition to perceiving what goes on within the mind and in the outer world, has the function of controlling voluntary motor activity. Since the system *Pcs.*, as we have noted, normally controls access to the system *Cs.*, it follows that it is the system *Pcs.* which normally has control of external perception, of action, and of conscious awareness. It maintains its control by means of the intersystemic censor, i.e., by repression, and in this sense the censor is the guardian of mental health, as noted above. As long as the censor functions efficiently, the wishes of the system *Ucs.* and the mental energy associated with them cannot become conscious or influence behavior unless they first become preconscious and thereby subject to the controlling influences of realistic, logical, and moral considerations. Only if repression fails, can instinctual wishes gain partial or complete control of conscious thought and of motor behavior.

This outline of the functions of the systems *Ucs.*, *Pcs.*, and *Cs.*, as well as of the relations of the three systems with one another will suffice for our present purpose. We have attempted to pay particular attention in the course of our outline to the explanations offered by the topographic theory for the clinically observable data concerning intrapsychic conflict, since, as we shall see, it was precisely in this area that Freud eventually found the topographic theory to be inadequate.

3

Freud's Criticisms of the Topographic Theory

IN THIS CHAPTER we shall discuss Freud's reasons for dissatisfaction with certain aspects of the topographic theory, reasons which led him to discard the topographic theory and to substitute the structural theory for it. The principal source for the material of this chapter will be *The Ego and the Id* (1923a), since it is in that monograph that Freud set forth his reasons for making the change just referred to.

In our presentation of the elements of the topographic theory we emphasized the importance which Freud placed on the idea that one of the prime requisites of an acceptable theory of mental functioning is that it must offer a satisfactory explanation of intrapsychic conflict. His clinical experience had convinced him, first, that a conflict between sexual wishes and repressive forces underlies every neurotic symptom; and, second, that the same conflict is responsible for the resistance which invariably appears in every psychoanalysis and which is the chief source of the various technical problems with which the analyst must deal. We are already familiar with the way in which the topographic theory explains such conflicts. According to it, conflicts within the mind take place between the system *Ucs.* and the system *Pcs.* More specifically, any such conflict takes place between a sexual wish of the system *Ucs.* which is inaccessible to consciousness and the realistic and moral standards of the system *Pcs.* The system *Pcs.* seeks to repress the offensive sexual wish. If it is successful in doing so, the wish becomes a part of the repressed and the conflict is solved for the time being. It is only when repression fails that the repressed wish returns from repression and forces its way into conscious life as a neurotic symptom despite the continued opposition of the system *Pcs.* A word should be added here about the role of anxiety in intrapsychic conflict as it was understood in the framework of the topographic theory. Freud's position (Brenner, 1955a, 1957) was that neurotic anxiety (as opposed to realistic anxiety caused by an external danger) results from a failure of repression. The fact that a sexual wish or a sexual experience is accompanied by anxiety rather than by pleasurable excitement or gratification is a sign that repression has taken place. Thus repression precedes neurotic anxiety and creates the conditions which make it possible for neurotic anxiety to develop.

What were the clinical data which convinced Freud that the explanation which the topographic theory offers of intrapsychic conflict is unsatisfactory? What were the observations that convinced him of the need to revise the topographic theory into what we know as the structural one?

The two observations which Freud emphasized in *The Ego and the Id* (1923a) were (1) that in neurotic conflicts the forces within the mind which oppose the sexual wishes in question are by no means always readily accessible to consciousness; and (2) that a need for punishment likewise may often be quite inaccessible to consciousness, or accessible to it only with great difficulty.

[25]

We propose to consider each of these observations in turn and in some detail so as to clarify as much as possible the difficulties which each observation presents when one attempts to explain it by means of the topographic theory.

1. At the close of the first chapter of *The Ego and the Id* Freud illustrated the fact that anti-instinctual forces within the mind are often inaccessible to consciousness by the following example. When an unconscious wish becomes active in the mind of a patient in analysis as he is lying on the couch, it ordinarily makes itself known through its influence on his associations. If the wish is not a repressed one, the patient will express it more and more directly and will soon become himself aware of it. If, however, the wish is a repressed one, instead of expressing his wish more directly and becoming aware of it, at a certain point the patient will fall silent or change the subject. It is clear to the analyst that the patient is resisting talking about the repressed wish. The patient himself, however, is quite unaware that he is trying to avoid saying something or to avoid thinking about something, i.e., that he is engaged in repressing a wish which, if he did not repress it, would become conscious. Moreover, it requires special work on the part of both the analyst and the patient before the patient can become aware that he is in fact resisting something, work which today we subsume under the heading of defense analysis, or, more generally, of ego analysis.

These facts are easy to observe and familiar to all analysts. What implications do they have for theory? In what way or ways do they contradict the topographic theory?

The contradiction is this. According to the topographic theory, the repressing agency of the mind is the censor of the system *Pcs*. Since it belongs to that system it should, by definition, be readily accessible to consciousness. The topographic theory makes no provision for the fact that mental forces which are responsible for repression can be inaccessible to consciousness, or accessible to it only with the help of analytic work. On the contrary, as we have seen, according to the topographic theory, anything active in the mind which is inaccessible to consciousness and which can be made conscious only by analysis must belong to the system *Ucs*. It could not possibly belong to the system *Pcs*. By the same token, still according to the topographic theory, it cannot be an anti-instinctual or repressing element of the mind. It must be a repressed sexual wish. Here then is a clear contradiction between fact and theory. Theory says that whatever is inaccessible to consciousness must be a repressed, sexual wish of the system *Ucs*. The fact is, however, that an anti-instinctual, repressing mental activity of the mind may be inaccessible to consciousness as well.

Freud expressed the dilemma by saying that it was clear that the fact that something in the mind is inaccessible to consciousness cannot be made, "as we should have hoped to do, the basis of far-reaching and inevitable conclusions" (1923a, p. 18). In other words, whether something is accessible or inaccessible to consciousness cannot profitably be used as the basis for dividing the mental apparatus into systems. For such a division to be profitable or useful in psychoanalysis it has to conform to the facts of mental conflict. In 1900 Freud's attention as a clinician was focused on repressed sexual wishes. At that time it was quite acceptable in light of his experience to equate what was inaccessible to consciousness with what derived from or was closely associated with sexual wishes. Thus, according to the topographic theory, the infantile, sexual elements of the mind are inaccessible to consciousness and comprise the system *Ucs*. In situations of mental conflict these mental elements are opposed

[27]

and censored by the more adult, realistic, and moral elements of the mind which are accessible to consciousness and which comprise the system *Pcs*. By 1923, however, his attention had been engaged by the task of scrutinizing in detail the anti-instinctual forces of the mind as well as the instinctual ones. His scrutiny of these had shown him that anti-instinctual forces, too, can be inaccessible to consciousness. If the mind is divided into systems on the basis of accessibility to consciousness, then mental conflict cannot be described as a conflict between two systems of the mind, i.e., between the systems *Ucs*. and *Pcs*. What is inaccessible to consciousness is not identical with what is instinctual. It includes at least some of what is anti-instinctual as well. What is important to realize in all this is that Freud considered the decisive reason for discarding the topographic theory to be the recognition that it did not offer an adequate explanation of mental conflict. It seems as though he reasoned in this way. As clinicians we see that the centrally important factor in mental life is conflict. In conflict one group of mental functions or tendencies is in opposition to another group. Any theory we have of the mental apparatus must give this fact first place. If we are to divide the mental apparatus into separate parts, the division must be along the lines of cleavage which are apparent in conflict; otherwise our theoretical division is of no use to us just where we need it the most in our practice. What we need in our practice is a theory that will help us to understand, to study, and to treat situations of intrapsychic conflict. Unless a theory takes conflict as its starting point therefore, it is not likely to be of much use to us.

2. The second of the two observations in *The Ego and the Id* which runs counter to the ideas of the topographic theory and which required a change in that theory is that a need or tendency to punish oneself may be inaccessible to con-

seiousness (1923a, p. 49ff.). According to the topographic theory, a moral trend, such as a need for punishment, should be a part of the system *Pcs.*, should be arrayed with the anti-instinctual forces of the mind in situations of conflict over sexual wishes, and should, by those tokens, be readily accessible to consciousness. To find that a need for punishment may be quite inaccessible to consciousness therefore raises all the objections to the topographic theory that we have just discussed in connection with unconscious repressive forces in general.

However, there is an additional problem in connection with a need for punishment which is inaccessible to consciousness. Freud pointed out that hysterical patients may actually repress self-punitive tendencies (1923a, p. 51). He likewise noted that it is characteristic in cases of obsessional neurosis for the repressive forces of the mind to wage a battle on two fronts: against sadomasochistic wishes on the one hand and against self-punitive and self-accusatory tendencies on the other. The validity of these observations has been amply confirmed in subsequent years. Indeed Fenichel (1945) strongly emphasized the importance of what we should, in the language of the structural theory, call defenses against self-punitive and self-accusatory tendencies and asserted that no case of obsessional neurosis can be successfully analyzed without analysis of this particular aspect of the patient's mental conflict.

What this means is that intrapsychic conflict does not consist only of conflict between sexual wishes on the one hand and anti-instinctual forces on the other. There can also be conflicts between a need for punishment on the one hand and counterforces, e.g., repression, on the other hand. Moreover, these conflicts can be of pathogenic significance and may consequently require analysis in the therapeutic situation, analysis which today we should call superego analysis.

Conflicts of this sort cannot be satisfactorily accounted for within the conceptual framework of the topographic theory except by assuming that they occur within the system *Pcs*. Even then, however, one could not explain the fact that they are inaccessible to consciousness without analytic work, something which, by definition, ought to assign them to the system *Ucs*.

Here then are two reasons which convinced Freud that the topographic theory must be changed, i.e., that accessibility to consciousness could no longer be kept as the central concept in organizing a theory of the mental apparatus. First, anti-instinctual forces may be as inaccessible to consciousness as are the sexual wishes they repress. Incidentally, Freud himself called this reason for changing his theory the decisive one. Second, a need for punishment may itself be a source of conflict and may be repressed in the same way as a sexual wish.

4

The Structural Theory

SINCE THERE ARE several expositions and discussions of the structural theory in the literature (Freud, 1923a, 1926, 1932a, 1940; A. Freud, 1936; Hartmann, Kris, and Loewenstein, 1946; Brenner, 1955a), in this chapter we shall limit ourselves to a brief summary of the principal features of that theory.

We have already discussed the considerations which led Freud to formulate the structural theory, namely, that the topographic theory does not correspond to certain of the facts of mental conflict which are observable. The structural theory was intended to achieve the correspondence which the topographic theory lacks. It divides the mind in accordance with Freud's experience as to which mental functions are generally allied with one another in situations of mental conflict and which are opposed to one another. Thus the major division of the mind is into two parts. One part, called the id, is directly related to the instinctual drives, while the other part, called the ego, is more coherent and more organized. It regulates or opposes the drives, mediating between them and the demands of the external world. This division corresponds to what one can observe of how the mind functions in situations of conflict over an instinctual drive. On the one side in such a conflict is the instinctual wish with its

[31]

associated fantasies and memories. On the other side are the anti-instinctual forces of the mind, both moral and defensive. The structural theory makes a second division within the ego itself, separating from the rest of the ego those functions which may be called the moral ones. They are called the superego. This division corresponds to those conflicts over self-punitive trends which we noted in Chapter 3.

The structural theory then divides the mind into three groups of functions called the id, the ego, and the superego. The division is made in such a way that the principal sorts of mental conflicts with which we are familiar can be described as occurring between id on the one hand and ego and superego on the other, or between ego and superego. Each group of functions is often called a mental structure, whence the name, the structural theory. Let us now consider in somewhat more detail each of the three mental structures which are distinguished by the structural theory.

THE ID

The id consists of the mental representatives of the instinctual drives. As such it is the great source of mental energy for the whole of the mental apparatus. The wishes of the id press for gratification and in so doing they impel the functions of the ego to action. As we shall see when we come to discuss the ego, this action may be of various kinds. The point is that the impulse and the energy for the ego come from the id.

The energy of the id is assumed to be of two kinds, in accordance with the dual instinct theory (Freud, 1920): aggressive energy, deriving from the aggressive instinct, and libido deriving from the erotic instinct. Since these two kinds of energy are assumed to be never wholly separate from each other but rather to be always fused, though in varying proportions, the cathexes of the instinctual wishes and fantasies of the id are partly aggressive and partly libidinal. That is to say, however destructive, cruel, and aggressive a particular fantasy or action may be, analysis will show it aims at some degree of erotic gratification as well. By the same token, no matter how loving and tender a fantasy or action may be, if it can be analyzed, analysis will show that there is at the same time some element of aggressive energy which is also being discharged.

The cathexes of the id are mobile and press for immediate and rapid discharge. Thus displacement and condensation characterize id processes, without, however, being limited to them, as we shall see later. A demand for immediate gratification likewise characterizes the id. This corresponds to the tendency of id cathexes to press for prompt and rapid discharge.

THE EGO

At the beginning of life the whole of the mental apparatus functions in the way just described as characteristic for the id. The mind of the infant is concerned solely with the task of discharging as promptly as possible the mobile cathexes of instinctual origin which energize it. Certain parts of the mind are of particular importance in executing this task, namely, the parts which subserve the functions of perception and of motor action. In other words, the infant achieves instinctual gratification with the help of his ability (1) to perceive the opportunities for gratification in his environment, e.g., an object to suck; and (2) to exploit those opportunities or physically to alter his environment, i.e., in the example just given, to bring the object he has perceived to his mouth. These perceptual and executant parts of the mind form the nucleus of the developing ego as the infant matures. Freud's (1923a, 1932a) formulation of this relationship between id and ego was that at the beginning of life the id comprises the whole of the mind and that the ego represents that part of the mind which develops under the impact of sensory stimuli from the outer world. According to this formulation, the ego is, figuratively speaking, the differentiated, cortical layer of the id, the part of the id which is in contact with the outer world. Hartmann (1939a, 1950b) has since suggested that it is more appropriate to think of the infant's mind as an undifferentiated matrix which in the course of development differentiates into an executant part, the ego, and an energizing part, the id. This alternative formulation takes into account in a more explicit way the fact that the sensory and motor apparatuses of the body, as well as the mental functions of perception and motor action from which the ego later develops, are distinguishable even at the beginning of life from the instinctual drives and their activities, just as the ego is later distinguishable from the id. In any case, it is clear that the early relationship between the id and the developing ego is that the latter is the executant for the former by virtue of being the part of the mind which achieves and maintains contact with the outer world.

The role which the ego plays in mental life is one which develops gradually. At first the ego is represented by a group of sensory and motor functions which act as the dutiful servants of the id and as its ambassadors to the outside world, so to speak. After a few years a marked change has taken place. In addition to its original role as executant for the id drives, the ego is able to exercise at least a modicum of control over instinctual wishes and may even oppose them directly in situations of conflict by using such measures as repression. The precise ways in which this change comes about are not easy to specify in detail (cf. Brenner, 1955a, Ch. 3). It seems certain that many factors are involved in the development of the ego into a coherent organization of mental functions. One of these factors is maturation of the nervous system. Without it even so basically important a function as voluntary motor control, for example, could not develop, since we know that the corticospinal tracts become myelinated and able to function only some months after birth. For many other ego functions as well, the nervous system must mature postnatally before the mental activity in question becomes possible. Equally indispensable to normal ego development are what we call good early object relations. By this we mean a set of experiences with the persons of his environment which afford the infant gratification and frustration in suitable or favorable proportions (Spitz, 1945; Kris, 1950b). The effect of such object relations is manifold as far as ego development is concerned (Hartmann, 1950a; Beres and Obers, 1950). Among other things they are important for the vitally significant identifications which result from them. A particularly significant step in ego development is the acquisition of language, a process which results in an incalculable facilitation of thought, as Freud remarked. The gradual acquisition of the ability to test reality, i.e., to distinguish between environmental fact and inner fantasy, should also be mentioned in connection with ego development, as should the acquisition of a store of memories and the gradual achievement of motor control. The capacity to delay the process of instinctual discharge is an attribute of ego functioning which also deserves special mention because of its general importance in the way the ego operates. Freud considered it to be the one attribute which most characteristically distinguishes ego from id. In par-

[35]

ticular, it is of special importance in the development of thinking, an ego function which Freud described as trial action, i.e., a delay in the discharge of all but a small amount of available mental energy.

All of these factors, and many others, are of very great importance in ego development, but the factor which is of crucial importance in the development of *conflict* between ego and id, and in the ability of the ego to oppose the instinctual drives, is anxiety (Freud, 1926). The relation between anxiety and conflict may be summarized as follows. We have observed earlier that the accumulation of instinctual energy within the mind produces unpleasure and leads to mental activity which is directed toward discharging the energy in question or toward binding it. If, however, the amount of instinctual energy which has accumulated is too great for the mental apparatus to deal with it either by binding it or by discharging it, a state of intense unpleasure results. Freud called such an event a traumatic event and the resultant state a traumatic state. He identified the emotion which accompanies a traumatic state as anxiety. Traumatic states are most apt to occur in infancy and in early childhood when the ability of the mental apparatus to bind and to discharge energy efficiently and without outside help is not yet well developed. Later on, as the ego develops, the individual's capacity to deal with large amounts of mental energy increases greatly.

Freud noted that there are certain situations which are apt to occur in every child's life and which lead to the development of a traumatic state. The first of these, which is most important in very early life, is the absence of the child's mother. The second, which is of prime importance at a slightly later time of life, is a situation in which the parent punishes or scolds the child, so that the latter fears his parent no longer loves him. The third, which is characteristic of the oedipal period, is a fantasy of castration in the case of a little boy or an analogous fantasy in the case of a little girl. The fourth situation arises only after the establishment of the superego, which will be discussed later, and consists in disapproval by the superego and in the threat of punishment from it. These situations are recognized as the typical danger situations of childhood, so called because in each there is danger that a traumatic situation will develop. In each case the child's ego reacts with anxiety, i.e., with an anticipatory unpleasure to the recognition, based on past experience, that a traumatic situation may develop. Moreover, as the ego develops further the child recognizes that its own instinctual wishes may lead to one or another danger situation or to a traumatic state if a danger situation is already present. Thus certain instinctual wishes come to be sources of danger and of anxiety.

The way in which anxiety makes it possible for the ego to oppose an instinctual wish is this. Once the ego has reacted to an instinctual wish with anxiety, the pleasure principle comes into operation. As Freud emphasized, this principle dominates the operation of the child's mind. It compels the ego to oppose the wish which gave rise to anxiety (the anticipation of intense unpleasure) rather than to gratify it. Thus it is anxiety which is responsible for the appearance of conflict between id and ego in the course of every child's development. It is important to bear in mind that conflicts of this sort are not to be thought of as necessarily abnormal or pathological. On the contrary, while they play a fundamentally important role in pathological mental processes such as neurotic symptoms, they are also inevitable and significant factors in normal mental development and functioning.

The means which the ego employs to oppose id wishes are called defenses. Each is set in action by anxiety, i.e., each has as its aim to diminish or to avoid anxiety. Any means at the ego's command may be used as a defense. Thus, for example, heterosexuality may be used as a defense against homosexual wishes, or vice versa. Among the better known defenses are repression, isolation, undoing, reaction formation, denial, projection, identification, the substitution of oneself for an external instinctual object, and vice versa (A. Freud, 1936).

To sum up what we have just said about anxiety, conflict, and defense, (1) there are typical fears which motivate the institution of anti-instinctual defenses by the ego; (2) defenses are of many kinds; and (3) the consequences of conflict may be either normal or pathological. They include character traits, sublimations, and individual sexual patterns or preferences as well as such consequences of conflict as permanent blocking of an instinctual derivative (successful defense) and neurotic symptom formation (unsuccessful defense).

Let us turn now to other aspects of ego functioning.

Ego cathexes may be either mobile or bound. Mobility of cathexis is characteristic of ego functioning in infancy and in early childhood, as well as of those situations in later life in which ego functions are closely allied with id impulses and act as their executants, i.e., facilitate their discharge. An example of such a situation is sexual intercourse and orgasm. The capacity to bind mental energy increases as the child matures, reaching a maximum in adult life. It is closely associated with deinstinctualization or neutralization of mental energy (Hartmann, Kris, and Loewenstein, 1949), by which is meant deflection of energy from its original, instinctual, pleasure-seeking aims and utilization of it for ego functions which have no directly instinctual quality. An example is the mental energy used for speech. When the little child is in the process of learning to speak, he derives obvious pleasure from the mere activity of speaking or even of prattling. In later life, however, speaking is not ordinarily pleasurable in itself. It is an activity under the control of the ego which can be used in the service of the functions and aims of the ego, whether these aims are instinctual and pleasure-seeking or not. Among the ways by which energy can be neutralized and made available for ego activities, sublimation and identification occupy important places.

There is no complete list of ego functions. However, any attempt to formulate such a list would have to include the following: (1) consciousness; (2) sense perception; (3) the perception and expression of affect; (4) thought; (5) control of motor action; (6) memory; (7) language; (8) defense mechanisms and defensive activity in general; (9) control, regulation, and binding of instinctual energy; (10) the integrative and harmonizing function; (11) reality testing; and (12) the capacity to inhibit or suspend the operation of any of these functions and to regress to a primitive level of functioning (Kris, 1934; Hartmann, 1939a). Thought processes of the ego vary from logical, realistic, problem-solving to unrealistic, nonverbal daydreaming.

THE SUPEREGO

The superego may be defined as the group of mental functions which have to do with ideal aspirations and with moral commands and prohibitions. It owes its origin as an organized division of the mind to identification with parental figures, in particular to identification with their ethical and moral aspects. This identification is primarily a consequence of the violent mental conflicts of the phallic, oedipal phase of development. It is in fact one of the most important consequences of the oedipal phase.

Usually it is the oedipal rival who is the principal source of the identifications which comprise the nucleus of the superego. Thus the little boy identifies with the father, who, at least in the child's fantasy, threatens to castrate and send him away forever in retaliation for the child's oedipal wish to displace and castrate his father. By internalizing his father's threat and making it a part of his own mind, i.e., by identifying with this aspect of his father, the boy becomes more able to institute defenses against and thus to control his frightening incestuous and parricidal wishes. At the same time the identification gratifies the instinctual wish to share in the father's fantasied (sexual) omnipotence by merging with him, e.g., via a fantasy of oral incorporation.

One of the most striking characteristics of the superego and one which is particularly impressive in the pathological situations with which the analyst deals clinically is its cruel, relentless, and even destructive attitude toward the individual of whose mind it is a part. This is particularly apparent in depressed patients, in patients with obsessional neuroses, and in those patients whose mental lives are dominated by a need for punishment. Freud explained the aggressive or destructive nature of superego functioning as a consequence of identification. He postulated that identification results in a partial defusion of mental energy into libido and aggressive energy. In the case of superego formation, the aggressive energy which is liberated in this way becomes available to the superego and accounts for the superego's cruelty and destructiveness.

Freud conceived of the superego as a specialized part of the ego. It resembles the rest of the ego in that some of its elements are readily accessible to consciousness while others are not. It also resembles the rest of the ego in that superego ideation can vary from what is logical, consistent, and mature to what is primitive and infantile.

Superego activity may be manifest in a variety of ways. It may regulate ego activities and particularly the ego's anti-instinctual, defensive activities in accordance with its moral standards. In such a case there is harmony between ego and superego. In other cases there may not be complete harmony between the two. In such instances the superego functions so as to give rise to a feeling of guilt within the ego, or a feeling of remorse, or a desire to do penance or to make restitution. At other times it may motivate an individual to punish himself without knowing why he does so, or even, in many cases, without knowing that he is doing so.

FINAL COMMENT

Two important aspects of the structural theory are the emphasis which it places on the genetic or developmental aspect of mental functioning and what Waelder (1930) called the principle of multiple functioning.

According to the structural theory, those mental functions which are called the ego, which normally form a coherent and integrated whole, and which may be in conflict with either the id or the superego, develop from the apparatuses of the mind which have to do with an individual's response to the world about him. Thus the ego may be characterized in either of two ways. (1) It may be defined as a group of functions of the mind which are usually associated with one another in situations of mental conflict; or (2) it may be defined as the group of mental functions which in one way or another have to do with mediating between the demands of the id and those of the outer world. The structural theory calls explicit attention to the genetic relationship between ego functions in later life and those of infancy and child-hood. It particularly emphasizes the effects of early conflicts on later ego functions. The importance of such genetic relationships in practical analytic work is especially apparent with respect to the understanding of anxiety and defense in cases of pathogenic conflict in later life.

The superego likewise is defined in the structural theory on a genetic basis as well as on a functional one. From the latter point of view it may be defined as the group of mental functions having to do with ideal aspirations and with moral prohibitions. From the former, it is definable as the consequence of certain oedipal identifications, namely, of identification with the moral aspect of the parents. Here again the structural theory's emphasis on the genetic point of view is of very great practical importance in actual analytic work with patients.

As for multiple function, according to the structural theory, any product of mental activity is invariably multiply determined (Waelder, 1930). This is true whether the product is a thought, an action, a fantasy, or a symptom. Whatever it may be, it is the outcome of a mutual interaction among tendencies of id, ego, and superego. At times these tendencies reinforce one another, at other times they cooperate, at still other times they oppose one another. In any case, each contributes its share to the final outcome.

5

Comparison of the Two Theories

In this chapter we propose to compare the structural and the topographic theories. We shall discuss both the similarities between them and the points of difference. In doing so we hope to be able to demonstrate the correctness of our introductory assertion that the two theories are in fact incompatible with each other and that one cannot use them interchangeably, as is usually maintained.

DIFFERENCES BETWEEN THE TWO THEORIES

1. The principle which the topographic theory uses to divide the mental apparatus is that of accessibility to consciousness, a principle which is reflected in the very names of the system *Ucs.*, *Pcs.*, and *Cs.* The basis for using this principle is the idea that mental conflict, when it occurs, is between what is accessible to consciousness and what is inaccessible to it. According to the topographic theory, the instinctual aspect of mental conflict is inaccessible to consciousness, while the anti-instinctual aspect is accessible to consciousness. The structural theory, on the other hand, divides the mind on a quite different basis into an instinctual part, a part which comprises the moral functions, and a part which mediates among the first two parts and the outer

[43]

world. The structural theory divides the mind in this way in order to conform more accurately to the clinical data concerning mental conflict: such conflicts occur typically between ego and superego as well as between id and ego plus superego. Moreover, the relationship between conflict and accessibility to consciousness is both more complex and more variable than what the topographic theory assumes it to be, as we have seen. What is instinctual may sometimes be accessible to consciousness, while what is anti-instinctual is very often inaccessible to consciousness without analytic work.

2. The topographic theory, in accordance with the assumptions just mentioned, asserts that in situations of conflict the anti-instinctual forces act so as to bar the instinctual elements from access to consciousness. Defense is thus synonymous with repression. According to the structural theory, repression is one among many defense mechanisms. Some of these, like isolation and undoing, do not involve barring instinctual derivatives from access to consciousness, as repression does. Moreover, the ego may utilize for defensive purposes whatever is available to it, even instinctual gratification, as we have noted.

3. According to the topographic theory, repression creates the situation which makes possible the development of neurotic anxiety. If repression fails, the repressed libido may be transformed into neurotic anxiety. Thus repression precedes the development of neurotic anxiety and is the precondition for it. On the other hand, the structural theory views anxiety as the motive for repression or for any other defense. The ego institutes a defense against an id impulse because it anticipates that that impulse, if gratified, would lead to a traumatic state. Thus, according to the structural theory, (a) anxiety is an anticipation of danger, whether real or

[44]

fantasied; and (b) anxiety precedes defense, not the other way around.

4. Both the structural and the topographic theories assume that psychic energy derives from the instinctual drives. However, the psychoanalytic theory of the drives changed radically in 1920 with the publication of *Beyond the Pleasure Principle,* and the relation of this change to the introduction of the structural theory is a significant one. Prior to 1920 the instinctual drives comprised the sexual or libidinal drives and the ego drives. Thereafter they were divided into libidinal and aggressive drives. On purely formal or logical grounds the change in the theory of drives seems not related to the change in the theory of the mental apparatus which followed it by three years. It might have been possible for Freud to have introduced aggression as an independent drive within the framework of the topographic theory without violating the requirements either of logic or of internal consistency, though it would have been difficult for him to do so (Hartmann, 1948). In fact, however, it seems likely that the introduction of the concept of an aggressive drive was closely related to the innovations concerning the psychic apparatus which are contained in *The Ego and the Id,* even though Freud himself did not explicitly establish the connection. The importance of self-directed, destructive tendencies had become increasingly clear to Freud from 1915 on (see, for example, "Mourning and Melancholia," 1917b), and the conclusion seems inescapable that it was the observation of these tendencies in man's mental life that led to the theory of the aggressive drive on the one hand and of the superego on the other. If this assumption is true, the difference between the structural and the topographic theories with respect to the role of aggression in mental life is not merely an incidental one. It would seem rather to be intimately related to a pro-

found and real difference between the two: the importance and the mode of action of self-directed aggression are fundamental to those parts of the structural theory which concern the superego, while they play no comparable part in the topographic theory (Arlow, 1956).

5. The topographic theory conceives of the mental apparatus as analogous to a reflex arc. This analogy, which was pictorialized in the familiar illustrations in Chapter VII of *The Interpretation of Dreams,* has been a source of some trouble and confusion, as Fisher (1957), for example, has noted. The diagram places the system *Pcs.* at the motor end of the apparatus, yet as Freud himself makes clear in the accompanying text, the system *Pcs.* exercises various of its functions at the sensory end of the apparatus as well, a concept which contradicts the analogy to a reflex arc. Moreover, adherence to this analogy resulted in postulates concerning the normal direction of the flow of energy within the apparatus which are difficult to reconcile with each other: the normal course of excitation is sensory to motor, yet in early life excitations deriving from the system *Ucs.* are assumed to pass normally to the sensory end of the apparatus as well and to result in the phenomenon commonly known as a hallucinated wish fulfillment. The structural theory has abandoned the analogy between the psychic apparatus and the reflex arc. By doing so it avoids the inner inconsistencies and opportunities for confusion which arise from the concept of a forward and backward course of energic flow within the mental apparatus. The significance of this change will appear in more detail in the subsequent chapters on regression and on the relation of dream psychology to the structural theory.

6. Although Freud (1900) recognized from the start that the system *Pcs.* develops gradually in the course of growing

up, relatively little emphasis is placed on this idea and little attention is paid to it in the topographic theory. The structural theory, on the other hand, emphasizes the gradual maturation and development of ego functions and their gradual integration into a functional unity, the ego. It also emphasizes the genesis and gradual development of the superego. In other words, genetic factors and the genetic viewpoint in general occupy a more important place in the structural theory than in the topographic one. They are relatively more important in the former than they are in the latter. This difference between the two theories, though only one of degree, seems to us to have been decisive in leading the way to a more adequate understanding of such important mental phenomena as regression and the primary and secondary processes.

7. There is another difference between the two theories which seems to us to be an important one even though it might be considered to be only a matter of difference in emphasis like the one just mentioned. This difference concerns the idea of multiplicity of causal factors in mental life. Within the framework of the topographic theory this idea occupies an important position, but a somewhat limited one. It is represented by two concepts, that of compromise formation and that of overdetermination. Of the two, the concept of compromise formation seems to be somewhat the more important, since every neurotic symptom, for example, is understood as a compromise formation between a sexual wish which has escaped from repression and the censor of the system *Pcs.* Overdetermination is a somewhat different concept. If a dream, for instance, represents the fulfillment of two or three wishes of the system *Ucs.*, wishes which are not particularly related to one another, but which are merely severally satisfied by the same dream, that dream is said to

be overdetermined. It has not one correct meaning which can be interpreted with proper technique but two or more independent meanings. It is similarly possible for a neurotic symptom or for a parapraxis to be overdetermined. Within the framework of the structural theory, however, the idea of a multiplicity of causal factors plays a much larger role. Since Waelder (1930) first called attention to this aspect of mental functioning it is recognized that every action, every thought, every mental act is the result of a compromise or interaction among the various functions of the mind, i.e., among id, superego, and ego. Every action, every fantasy, every dream, every symptom will be a compromise or resultant of instinctual wishes, of moral demands or prohibitions, of defenses, of external factors, and so forth. A correct understanding of this principle of multiple functioning is essential to the proper application of the concepts of the structural theory to both clinical and theoretical problems. Though it is not new in principle, any more than is the genetic approach, it plays a much more significant role in the structural theory than in the topographic one.

So much for the major differences between the two theories.

SIMILARITIES BETWEEN THE TWO THEORIES

1. Basic to both theories is the idea that it is appropriate and advantageous to isolate from among the many contents and processes of the mind a particular group to be called the psychic or mental apparatus. This apparatus is definable in terms of its functions, which are to deal with the energies within the mind and to facilitate or regulate their discharge. The structural and topographic theories are thus alike in that each is a theory of a mental apparatus.

2. In discussing the differences between the two theories

we have emphasized the significance of the introduction of the concept that mental energies are basically of two kinds, libidinal and aggressive. With this important exception, however, the structural and topographic theories are alike with respect to their ideas concerning mental energy. Both theories assume that mental energy can be either free or bound, that the capacity to delay its discharge increases as the individual matures, and that when mental energy is bound the energic level of the mind is raised, a phenomenon which permits the mental apparatus to function more precisely as well as more effectively. In short, the libido theory in all its essentials is common to both the structural and the topographic theory.

3. Having emphasized the differences between the two theories with respect to intrapsychic conflict, we should at this point stress the fact that despite their differences they have many similarities in this regard. According to both theories, intrapsychic conflicts underlie every neurotic symptom as well as many normal phenomena. Both theories emphasize the importance of the conflicts which occur between instinctual and anti-instinctual forces within the mind, and in both, repression and the mental agencies responsible for repression play an important part.

4. The two theories rest alike on the basic premises of psychic determinism and of the importance of unconscious mental processes. Likewise common to both are the concepts of overdetermination, of compromise formation, and of genetic determinants, although, as we have noted, these last play a much larger role in the structural than in the topographic theory.

DISCUSSION AND CONCLUSIONS

We have discussed the similarities and the differences between the topographic and the structural theories. Both are

[49]

psychoanalytic theories. They have more in common with each other than either one of them has with any nonpsychoanalytic theory of human mental functioning. Why then do we maintain that the two theories are incompatible and that the structural theory is the superior one?

To begin with, the two theories are not only dissimilar but in many respects are actually contradictory. It may be helpful to consider these facts again. The topographic theory divides the functioning of the mental apparatus according to the criterion of accessibility to consciousness. Mental elements which are inaccessible to consciousness belong together and comprise the system *Ucs.* Such elements are instinctual in nature and primitive in origin. They follow the laws of the primary process and they are allied as a system in situations of mental conflict. The system *Pcs.,* on the other hand, is made up of elements which are readily accessible to consciousness. The contents of the system *Pcs.* are anti-instinctual in nature. They originate later in life and they operate according to the laws of the secondary process. In situations of conflict, the derivatives of the system *Ucs.* are opposed by the censor of the system *Pcs.* This is the manner in which mental conflict is delineated within the framework of the topographic theory.

According to the propositions of the structural theory, the topographic delineation of conflict as outlined above is only a rough and inaccurate approximation of the true state of affairs. It presents a picture which can be misleading and contradictory.

We should like to illustrate this last contention by presenting the following considerations.

1. Pathogenic conflicts do not represent exclusively the opposition between unconscious instinctual demands and the opposing anti-instinctual forces of the system *Pcs.* Con-

flicts may occur over moral demands. Conflicts may also occur as a consequence of the pressure from reality. The view of intrapsychic conflict as presented by the topographic theory does not give these elements sufficient weight. The topographic theory presents an oversimplified and inexact picture of mental functioning during conflict. In the structural theory, conflicts over moral demands are accounted for in terms of the superego. In addition, the structural theory makes proper allowance for the ego's orientation toward reality.

2. Derivatives of the drives may be *accessible* to consciousness. Memories of traumatic events which occurred in childhood can often be recalled quite readily (Freud, 1926). On the other hand, anti-instinctual forces, like defenses, may be *inaccessible* to consciousness (Freud, 1923a). According to the topographic theory, in the examples just given, the drive derivatives should belong to the system *Pcs.*, and the anti-instinctual defenses should belong to the system *Ucs.* Accordingly, the congruence between instinctual and unconscious on the one hand, and anti-instinctual and preconscious on the other hand, breaks down.

3. Moral demands may be conscious or unconscious. If viewed strictly within the framework of the topographic theory, such demands would fall at times within the province of the system *Pcs.* and at other times within the province of the system *Ucs.* In other words, if one uses the criterion of accessibility to consciousness, moral demands might at one time be considered to be allied to instinctual forces and at other times to anti-instinctual forces. According to the structural theory, however, moral demands are part of one system, the superego. The functioning of the superego, like that of any other part of the mental apparatus, may sometimes occur within the realm of consciousness and on other occasions

[51]

outside the realm of consciousness. Thus the structural theory resolves many of the contradictions which are inherent in the topographic theory.

4. Similar difficulties apply to the placing of unconscious fantasies into a particular system in the topographic theory. Because they are not accessible to consciousness and have the power to produce derivatives, such fantasies should belong to the system *Ucs*. On the other hand, unconscious fantasies are composed of definite word and object representations which may be integrated according to the laws of the secondary process. According to these criteria, such fantasies should belong to the system *Pcs*. In unconscious fantasies Freud (1915b) recognized a significant element of mental life whose functioning contradicted the essential criteria of the topographic theory.

As Freud (1915b) remarked, accessibility to consciousness is not a good criterion on which to build psychological systems. It was because of these considerations that he proposed to substitute for the topographic theory the structural theory, and to replace the guiding principle of accessibility to consciousness by the principle of conflict of functions among the drives, morality, reality, and the ego. The topographic theory was not simply enlarged to include structural concepts, it was fundamentally changed.

What are the practical consequences of this fundamental change of theory in psychoanalysis? To what extent does it influence the manner in which the clinician conducts his daily analytic work? The effect of this change of theory on psychoanalytic technique has been enormous. This point has been emphasized by many authors, e.g., Alexander (1930), Freud (1932a), A. Freud (1936), W. Reich (1945), Fenichel (1939), Hartmann (1951), Kris (1951), Loewenstein (1951), R. Sterba (1934), Arlow (1961). These are only a few of those who have written about the changes wrought in clinical practice by the introduction of the structural theory.

The situation may be summarized in the statement that, using the structural theory, the very nature of the therapeutic task has changed. According to the topographic theory, symptom formation is the result of failure of repression. There is a threatened irruption of unconscious, instinctual wishes into consciousness. These derivatives are barred from consciousness; and in the ensuing conflict, disguised, substitute expressions of the wish are discharged in the form of symptoms. The technical task in therapy is to abrogate repression, to recover the forgotten material, in particular the memory of childhood traumata. Essentially, the therapeutic task in the topographic sense is to make the unconscious conscious.

Matters are viewed much differently from the structural point of view. The structural theory takes account of the fact that intrapsychic conflict is much more than a problem of accessibility to consciousness, as the topographic theory assumes it to be. To be sure, the structural theory still considers the basis of symptom formation to be a failure of defense with resultant compromise formation. The structural theory, however, takes into account certain important clinical data which the topographic theory cannot account for. The first of these is the fact that not every defense acts in such a way as to bar drive derivatives from access to consciousness. In other words, repression is not the only defense. Moreover, since the defenses themselves are not always accessible to consciousness, the analysis of these defenses becomes a part of the therapeutic work. The purpose of technical intervention is no longer synonymous with the recovery of amnestic material, important though such recovery is. Nor can defenses be simply abrogated or circumvented to get at the instinctual derivatives which they are warding off. The therapeutic task aims at analyzing defenses, resolving their automatic operation, and permitting the integration of previously warded-off instinctual derivatives and the memories associated with them into the normal parts of the ego. This change in the therapeutic task was expressed by Freud epigramatically. Originally he said that the therapeutic task of psychoanalysis is to make the unconscious conscious. After the introduction of the structural theory he expressed the therapeutic goal in the words, "Where id was, there shall ego be."

Nor should the analysis of id derivatives and ego defenses be considered the total task in treatment according to the structural theory. Since the functioning of the superego may be conscious or unconscious, considerable analytic effort has to be expended to delineate and clarify moral demands and to demonstrate the role which they play in symptom and character formation. As indicated in Chapter 6, the regressive transformation of superego derivatives often makes the functioning of the superego seem as impulsive and as intractable as derivatives of the id. The resolution of automatic punitive demands of the superego in favor of the exercise of rational value judgments by the ego constitutes an additional dimension of technique which has been introduced with the structural theory. In other words, the structural theory makes clear to us the great importance of analyzing whatever *superego* manifestations are part of the pathogenic conflict. Finally, Freud's (1926) revision of the theory of anxiety, which followed the introduction of the structural theory and which was based upon it, altered still further our concept of the therapeutic task of analysis by adding to it the necessity of analyzing the motives of defense, i.e., the nature of the dangers which the ego's defenses are attempting to avoid.

We see therefore that the innovations of the structural theory concerning intrapsychic conflict and symptom formation result in a substantial revision of what the therapeutic task of analysis is considered to be. According to the topographic theory, the therapeutic task is essentially to make the patient conscious of the infantile, instinctual wishes which give rise to his pathogenic conflicts. According to the structural theory, it is important to make the patient conscious not only of the instinctual aspects of his conflicts but of their defensive and superego aspects as well, with careful attention to the content of the anxieties involved. All this is necessary in order to promote the integrative and controlling functions of the ego so that adequate discharge of instinctual energy, i.e., adequate instinctual gratification, is possible for the patient without symptom formation.

We hope we have succeeded in demonstrating clearly by comparing the two theories why they are not only different but incompatible, that is, contradictory in important respects. It is our contention that the topographic and the structural theories can neither be used interchangeably nor side by side. The structural theory alone is the proper basis for theoretical discussions as well as for psychoanalytic practice at present. In the chapters which follow we hope to elucidate certain of the consequences of adopting the structural theory which we believe have not yet been sufficiently recognized. In addition, we shall attempt to demonstrate its superiority over the topographic theory in various connections which we believe deserve emphasis.

6

The Concept of Regression and the Structural Theory

THE CONCEPT of regression was introduced into psychoanalysis as part of the topographic theory and was developed and applied in connection with that theory from its very beginnings. Even within the topographic hypothesis, however, several different meanings were accorded the notion of regression. As psychoanalytic theories developed, the idea of regression underwent considerable transformation. With the introduction of the structural hypothesis many aspects of the concept of regression, as used earlier, were continued within the new framework without revision or reconsideration. In this chapter we propose to examine what revision of the concept is necessary and desirable if we are to use the structural hypothesis in a consistent fashion.

HISTORICAL CONSIDERATIONS

The concept of regression was borrowed by Freud from two of his earliest and deepest interests, biology and neuropathology. The ideas of biological atavism and retrogression of morphological structures were characteristic of evolutionary biological thinking in the late nineteenth century. Freud had used these ideas in his early biological studies, but it is from the neurological theories of Hughlings Jackson that a direct line of influence on Freud's concept of regression may be discerned. Jackson's views are especially important because they emphasized functional retrogression as related to earlier stages of structural organization. Freud used these ideas in a very original fashion in his monograph, *On Aphasia* (1891). This monograph has been called by Bernfeld (1944) "the first psychoanalytic work." Concerning the phenomena of aphasia, Freud wrote, "In assessing the functions of the speech apparatus under pathological conditions we are adopting as a guiding principle Hughlings Jackson's doctrine that all these modes of reaction represent instances of functional retrogression (dis-involution) of a highly organized apparatus and therefore correspond to previous states of its functional development. This means that under all circumstances an arrangement of associations which, having been acquired later, belongs to a higher level of functioning, will be lost, while an earlier and simpler one will be preserved. From this point of view, a great number of aphasic phenomena can be explained" (p. 87).

The concept of genetic disinvolution became one of the cornerstones of psychoanalytic theory. It is still one of the fundamental conceptual tools which we use, but its meaning has changed over the years. Hartmann, Kris, and Loewenstein (1946) cite regression as an example of one of the working concepts of psychoanalytic theory which was borrowed from biology and which in the course of time acquired new meanings in the context in which it was used in psychoanalysis.

Within the topographic hypothesis the concept of regression was used in many senses: genetic, systemic, instinctual, phylogenetic, and biogenetic. Different meanings were accorded the term as it was used to explain a broader and broader range of clinical phenomena.

Actually the word "regression" was not introduced by Freud until the *Interpretation of Dreams*. Writing retrospectively, however, Freud (1914b) said that he came to realize during his early studies in hysteria that the backward turning in time of the patient's associations was a characteristic feature of the neuroses. It appeared to him that "psychoanalysis could explain nothing in the present without referring back to something past," and that an analytic technique which neglected regression would render scientific study of the neuroses impossible.[1]

It is in the description of the psychic apparatus in Chapter VII of the *Interpretation of Dreams* that the concept of regression takes on importance of the first magnitude. As a matter of fact, it was in the section titled "Regression" that Freud first described the topographic model of the mind. He used the idea of regression to explain why the wish-fulfilling tendency of mental life takes the form during sleep of a visual, hallucinatory experience, i.e., to explain how a dream is formed.

Freud began with the assumption that during the earliest phases of its existence the human mind reacts to situations of need or frustration by striving to experience once again a set of perceptions which it had previously experienced. These earlier perceptions had been connected with pleasurable gratification. The primordial tendency to bring about

[1] It may be remarked that Freud was here concerned with two aspects of psychoanalytic theory. The phenomena which he was describing were in part examples of regression and in part illustrations of the genetic determination of hysterical symptoms. This was not yet the concept of regression in its functional and instinctual context.

an identity of perception in the face of frustration results, said Freud, in a hallucinated wish fulfillment. Such a tendency, he continued, is dominant during infancy in waking life, and continues to be dominant in adult life during sleep. What a waking adult would ordinarily experience as a wishful thought, he experiences during sleep as a perception. His mental functioning has regressed to the type of functioning characteristic of infancy.

But in terms of his explanation of the relations between the different systems of the psychic apparatus, Freud also intended the term regression to signify a backward movement in a systemic or topographic sense. As has already been described (Chapter 2), Freud thought of the functions of the psychic apparatus as having a topographic or "spatial" relationship to each other. The mode of functioning of any mental content was assumed to depend upon its accessibility to consciousness. He postulated that in the ordinary course of mental functioning there is a predictable sequence of mental events from perception (the system $Cs.$) to memory (the system $Pcs.$) and in those instances which involve repression, to forgetfulness (the system $Ucs.$). Mental elements, grouped according to their accessibility to consciousness and sharing certain common functional features, constitute a system. As described in Chapter 2, the sequential relationship was compared to the reflex arc in which function is initiated at the sensory end by some perceptual experience, transmitted to appropriate, connecting intermediaries, and finally translated into motor action. Freud thought of the psychological wish as some sort of excitatory process originating in the system $Ucs.$, an energic tension which normally moves from the sensory end of the psychic apparatus toward discharge in appropriate activity at the motor end of the apparatus. He wrote, "The only way in which we can describe what happens in hallucinatory dreams is by saying that the excitation moves in a *backward* direction. Instead of being transmitted towards the *motor* end of the apparatus it moves towards the *sensory* end and finally reaches the perceptual system. If we describe as 'progressive' the direction taken by psychical processes arising from the unconscious during waking life, then we may speak of dreams as having a 'regressive' character" (1900, p. 542).

We see then that in 1900 Freud used the term "regression" in two distinct and parallel ways. He thought of regression in a genetic or temporal sense and at the same time used regression in a systemic sense, i.e., to designate a shift of predominance of functioning of one psychic system over another.[2]

A further dimension was added to the concept of regression with the discovery of infantile sexuality and with the introduction of the libido theory. This dimension was the notion of instinctual regression. The new contributions concerning the theory of instincts may be regarded as special elaborations of the topographic hypothesis, specifically of that highly important component of the mental apparatus, the system *Ucs.* According to the topographic theory, the system *Ucs.* is the oldest; it is the first to appear; and other systems develop out of it gradually, primarily as the result of conflict over frustrations of instinctual needs. The system *Ucs.* remains the great reservoir of the libidinal, instinctual wishes.

In *Three Essays on the Theory of Sexuality* (1905) Freud described the operation of sexual wishes in terms of the tendency for identity of perception referred to earlier, which

2 In the fourth edition (1914) of *The Interpretation of Dreams* Freud himself felt the need to explain that "regression" was used in several different meanings. In the fifth edition (1918), he added a paragraph on the concept of phylogenetic regression (1900, p. 548).

is characteristic of the system *Ucs*. He said, "The sexual aim of the infantile instinct consists in obtaining satisfaction by means of an appropriate stimulation of the erotogenic zone. . . . This satisfaction must have been previously experienced in order to have left behind a need for its repetition. . . . The state of being in need of a repetition of the satisfaction reveals itself in two ways: by a peculiar feeling of tension, possessing, rather, the character of unpleasure, and by a sensation of itching or stimulation which is centrally conditioned and projected on to the peripheral erotogenic zone. We can therefore formulate a sexual aim in another way: it consists in replacing the projected sensation of stimulation in the erotogenic zone by an external stimulus which removes that sensation by producing a feeling of satisfaction" (p. 184). In other words, under conditions of frustration libidinal wishes aim to achieve an identity of perception with memories of previous gratification. In waking life and normal development a real repetition of the perception of the previously experienced pleasurable sensation is effected. In the dream, during sleep, only a hallucinatory repetition of identity of perception is achieved. In either case, however, the *modus operandi* of the sexual wish is the same. It follows the functional tendencies of the system *Ucs*.

With the introduction of the libido theory, it became possible to extend the topographic hypothesis to include a description of the unfolding of the functioning of the system *Ucs*. and the relationship of this unfolding to the psychopathology of the neuroses. The three basic concepts which Freud used to explain this relationship are primal repression, fixation, and regression.

For a more detailed discussion of the relation between the first two of these concepts, i.e., primal repression and fixation, the reader is referred to Brenner (1957). At this point we may say merely that the two were conceived by Freud to be very closely related mechanisms, if not in fact identical. By means of them certain of the instinctual wishes of childhood, though repudiated by the developing system *Pcs.*, remain active (cathected) throughout life in the system *Ucs.* and constitute the nucleus of the repressed part of that system. When an instinctual or libidinal regression occurs in later life the libidinal cathexes regress to the fixation points already established within the system *Ucs.* Because of their increased cathexes, the previously repressed infantile wishes then break through the barrier of repression and give rise to neurotic symptoms.

Thus, according to Freud's theories after 1905, neurotic symptom formation is predicated on fixation and primal repression and is directly caused by libidinal regression. The two former mechanisms are assumed to lay the groundwork, and instinctual regression to cause the shift in equilibrium which results in the appearance of symptoms.

The specific character of a neurosis, moreover, is considered to depend directly upon the level of instinctual regression. What determines the clinical picture of obsessional neurosis, for example, was supposed to be the regression of the libido to the anal-sadistic stage. This was considered the predominating, if not the exclusive and essential element. What today we call the ego's mechanisms of isolation, reaction formation, and undoing, and the mental traits of ambivalence and magical thinking (all of which were known to Freud at the time) are regarded in this earlier formulation as the inevitable consequences of libidinal regression. What today we would regard as modes of ego functioning were assumed to be inevitably determined by their connection with a discrete libidinal phase.[3] Accordingly, if in the course of analysis one detected the operation of the process of conversion, it was taken for granted that the underlying conflict related to a typical, oedipal wish of the phallic phase. Recent investigators have adduced evidence to demonstrate that this is not always or necessarily the case (Fenichel, 1945; Marmor, 1953; Rangell, 1959).

The close connection between instinctual regression and the modes of ego function had far-reaching implications. Regression was generally conceived of as a global process. It was assumed that the entire personality regressed. It was thought, for example, that the obsessional patient treats all objects as if he unconsciously equated them with feces; or that sadomasochistic interests are the only interests of any consequence in the erotic life of such patients. Similarly, because depressions are based upon a regression to an oral instinctual fixation point, it was expected that the patient was returning to the oral phase of existence; in other words, that he was becoming in essence a helpless infant once again, experiencing all objects as breast or mother, and pursuing exclusively passive, dependent patterns of activity in all aspects of his life. It was as if one would say that the depressed person had become once again a suckling babe.

It is possible that this type of thinking is also responsible for another widespread misconception about the theory of regression (Arlow, 1963). We refer here to the idea that

3 Abraham (1924), for example, drew up a chart of libidinal development in which he meticulously detailed each successive layer of libidinal aim and object together with the mode of mental functioning associated with it. As Lewin (1950) has pointed out, Abraham, like Freud, had been a careful student of embryology, and there can be little doubt but that the influence of the idea of progressive development from antecedent germinal Anlagen may be discerned in his formulations. Conversely, regression was analogous to biological atavism and functional disinvolution.

derivatives of a particular instinctual wish must have originated during the phase in the individual's history when the
drive from which that wish derived was the dominant one
in mental life. Thus, for example, it has often been held that
an oral wish must have originated during the oral phase,
that is, during the first several months of life. This idea has
given rise to many misconceptions. The cannibalistic wish
to devour the father, for example, and thereby to acquire his
prowess, to become like him, and to take his place, is a
typical wish of the oedipal phase. It is true that it is an oral
wish, but it is quite different from those oral wishes which
engender conflicts in a psychotically depressed person. To
illustrate: a four-year-old boy was constantly play-acting and
indulging in fantasies of being a superman. He had always
enjoyed his food and had been a good eater. Suddenly he
began to gorge himself with marble cake. He explained his
behavior by saying that he wanted to eat lots of *marble* cake
in order to become like Captain *Marvel* (a superhuman,
story-book hero). Here we have an example of an oral wish
which serves the fulfillment of the typical, oedipal aim of
incorporating and supplanting the father. The fantasied
mode of incorporation is oral; its result is an identification
with the father.

Depressive conflicts originating in wishes from the "oral"
phase of development also involve cannibalism and incorporation, but if we follow the detailed description of these
early oral wishes as delineated by Lewin (1950), the differences become apparent at once. The wish to eat, to be eaten,
and to sleep serve the fulfillment of quite a different type
of fantasy, i.e., the achievement of a satiated, tension-free
fusion with the mother. As far as we can discern, it appears
that later derivatives of the triad of early oral wishes just
mentioned represent an attempt in later life to experience

perceptions identical with those which gave rise to pleasure during the first six months of life, i.e., during the oral phase. It is essential in clinical practice to distinguish between these different kinds of oral wishes. A wish for blissful union is very different from a wish to castrate and replace a rival. The two have different points of origin in the development of the individual. Though both are oral, they are not genetically the same.

To return to our main thesis, when the concepts of instinctual fixation and regression were introduced into psychoanalytic theory, the attention of analysts was directed chiefly to them. The other aspects of regression receded to the background. Regression came to be essentially synonymous with instinctual regression. Thus, for example, when Freud came to conceptualize the psychopathology of the psychoses, he did so in terms of a special type of libidinal regression. He attempted to explain the primary symptoms of psychosis as the consequences of regression to a very early phase of libidinal development which he called the phase of narcissism. The implications of this concept will be discussed more fully in Chapter 10, which deals with the psychopathology of the psychoses.

However, by 1913, Freud was already aware of certain of the difficulties which result from correlating regression with instinctual fixation alone. Some aspects of ego functioning, he felt, could and did develop independently of the instincts and their vicissitudes. In the Schreber case (1911b) he had suggested that the ego might play some role in determining the nature of regression. In the "Disposition to Obessional Neurosis" (1913a) Freud felt that the particular phase of development of the ego during which the inhibition of libidinal advance takes place should be taken into account in considering the choice of neurosis. He suggested that a

[65]

chronological outstripping of libidinal development by ego development should be included among the factors predisposing an individual to develop this type of neurosis.

Ferenczi (1913) went still farther in attempting to correlate the phenomena of the neuroses with ego development, at least in one area, the sense of reality. He suggested that with regression of the libido to earlier stages of development, the level of the reality sense that was dominant at the time of fixation also becomes renascent in the mechanisms of symptom formation. Thus, in hysteria, there is a regression of the reality sense to the stage of magical gestures (conversion), and in the obsessional neurosis, a regression to magical thinking (the omnipotence of thought characteristic of the auto-erotic or narcissistic phase of development).

These early works of Freud and Ferenczi mark the beginnings of the introduction of the concept of regression of ego functions into psychoanalytic theory as an addition to the well-established concept of instinctual regression. The first major step in this direction was made by Freud in connection with his analysis of delusions of being observed.

Freud (1914a, 1917b) explained that delusions of being watched constitute a regressive resolution of conscience into the historical events which gave rise to that agency.[4] They reveal how conscience originates from the moral teachings and prohibitions of parents and educators. In such delusions the censoring voices of the parents are reactivated from the store of memories and experienced once again as perceptions. In this instance, the reactivated perceptions belong almost

[4] Recent work suggests that some delusions of being watched are, as Freud proposed, related to regression of superego functions, while others represent regressive alterations of ego functions which are not particularly related to the superego (Modell, 1958).

exclusively to the sphere of auditory experience.[5] In normal mental functioning conscience is experienced as an *intrapsychic* relationship. In delusions of being observed, it is regressively re-experienced as an *interpersonal* relationship.

We can see that this explanation of a psychotic symptom departs somewhat from Freud's original explanation of symptom formation in psychosis. At first Freud (1911b) attributed symptom formation to instinctual regression, specifically to a regression to the narcissistic phase of libidinal organization. In his explanation of delusions of being watched Freud (1914a) emphasized an additional factor to explain the hallucinatory recapitulation of events from the subject's past experience. A regression of what we should now call certain ego functions has taken place, a regression of memory to perception, leading to a distortion of reality testing. This regression is not explained in terms of quantitative shifts of libido alone.

It will be recalled that one of the meanings of regression which we specified in Chapter VII of *The Interpretation of Dreams* was what we have called the genetic one: the revival of an earlier mode of functioning of the mental apparatus. We have pointed out that after 1905 this aspect of regression was largely overshadowed by the concept of instinctual regression. Here (1914) is the point in the development of Freud's theories at which the earlier meaning of regression began to re-emerge as a part of the newly developing concept of ego functions.[6]

5 This formulation is very like the concept of regression of mental function which Freud had applied to the problem of dream formation. The dream also constitutes a reactivation of certain impressions from the store of memories which are experienced in a hallucinatory way as perceptions. In the dream, however, the regressively reactivated memories or sensory impressions are predominantly, though by no means exclusively, visual in nature.

6 Hartmann (1956) noted that even in the Schreber case Freud (1911b, p. 79) had begun to perceive that libido development and ego development should be considered separately as well as in relation to each other.

Finally there are two other ways in which regression is used as an explanatory concept in psychoanalysis. These may be termed the phylogenetic and the biogenetic. Used in the phylogenetic sense, regression refers to those phenomena in mental life which represent man's archaic heritage psychically innate in him. According to this concept, certain forms of mental life reach back in their derivation beyond the childhood of the individual to the past of the race. Freud first introduced the concept of phylogenetic regression in the 1918 edition of *The Interpretation of Dreams*. He did so to indicate that memories of the race as well as memories of the individual may enter into the formation of a dream. It should be noted, however, that as early as 1912, Freud had adumbrated the notion of phylogenetic regression in his hypotheses concerning the origin of religion and social organization (1913b, p. 140ff.). In a similar vein (1921) he tried to explain the power which the hypnotist exerts over his subject as a reactivation of the relationship between the individual and the dreaded father of the primal horde. Phylogenetic regression was also adduced to account for the severity of castration anxiety and for its appearance in patients who had never experienced, as far as could be determined analytically, any actual threat of castration. Freud (1937-1939) suggested that the origin of castration anxiety and of the superego as a psychic institution could be traced to specific events in the history of the race. On an even broader sociological scale, such prehistoric memory traces were supposed to contribute their effects to the molding of national character and the repetitive upsurge of anti-Semitism throughout human history. Ferenczi (1924) made similar suggestions concerning the origin of the latency period in human sexual development. He thought that the interruption of the individual's sexual development during the latency period recapitulates

[68]

the interruption of evolutionary development that was occasioned by the appearance of the Ice Age. Investigating the clinical distortions of the sense of reality, Ferenczi (1913) spoke of a phylogenesis of the reality sense. He hoped that "we shall some day succeed in bringing the individual stages of the development of the ego, and the neurotic regression-types of these, into a parallel with the stages in the racial history of mankind" (p. 236). Daly (1943) tried to trace to racial experiences the origin of certain neurotic attitudes of men toward menstruation, and Nunberg (1947) pursued a similar course in his monograph on circumcision and problems of bisexuality.

In current psychoanalytic literature such use of the concept of regression is becoming less and less frequent, though one may still observe occasional references to phylogenetic regression. In general, we feel justified in saying that explanations based on regression to phylogenetic antecedents are nowadays regarded as hardly acceptable from the scientific point of view. In addition, there are often better explanations at hand to account for many phenomena for which the idea of phylogenetic regression is invoked.[7] Finally, there is a fundamental disadvantage in the use of the concept of phylogenetic regression. It is the type of argument which cannot be pursued investigatively. Such constructions, however suggestive, can be neither refuted nor validated by clinical data. Accordingly, they lose their usefulness as conceptual tools. When applied to the phenomena of mental life, phylogenetic regression contributes little more than a suggestive analogy.

The final form in which regression is used in psychoanalysis may be termed biogenetic regression. According to this

[7] Freud (1917c, 1932a), for example, as well as Hartmann and Kris (1945) have shown that determinants for castration anxiety may be demonstrated as occurring regularly in the child's actual experiences during the phallic period.

concept of regression, certain mental phenomena are supposedly derived from the evolutionary vicissitudes of subhuman forms of life. Such hypotheses go beyond individual ontogenesis and even phylogenesis. This type of regression is so far-reaching in its implications that one would hardly expect it to be used in modern psychoanalytic writings. As a matter of fact, however, regression in this sense is used as an explanatory concept more often than one suspects.

Numerous references could be quoted from the literature, but only a few illustrative examples need be referred to here. Even complicated ego functions or meticulously structured defenses have been explained on the basis of biogenetic regression. For example, self-castration, symbolic or actual, and organ alienation, have been related to the phenomenon of autotomy observed in salamanders (Fenichel, 1945; Rado, 1939). Trance states and stupors have been correlated to various innate instinctual reflex patterns observed in lower animals; and the masochistic character of female sexuality has been based, in at least one explanation, on the prototype of the "painful" penetration of the cell (Bonaparte, 1952).

The criticisms which were applied two paragraphs earlier to the use of phylogenetic regression could all be repeated with equal effect against the use of the concept of biogenetic regression. As a matter of fact, it should be emphasized that where it is possible to explain clinical data on the basis of ontogenetic formulations, the concepts of phylogenetic and biogenetic regression become unnecessary.

We have reviewed the various meanings which the word regression has had in the course of the development of psychoanalytic theory. We have described five different ways in which the term regression has been used—genetic, systemic, instinctual, phylogenetic, and biogenetic. Two of these, phylogenetic and biogenetic regressions, are of limited use scientifically and have no proper place in our current conceptual framework. Regression in the systemic sense is inconsistent with the structural theory. How then should the term regression be understood in our current frame of reference? What is the most useful and most accurate meaning to give to it at the present time?

MEANING OF REGRESSION IN THE STRUCTURAL THEORY

We may begin with the following general definition. Regression is the *re-emergence* of modes of mental functioning which were characteristic of the psychic activity of the individual during earlier periods of development. Viewed descriptively, regression may be regarded as primitivization of function (Kris, 1950a). This concept applies to the functioning of all parts of the psychic apparatus, to the instinctual drives of the id, to the modes of operation of the ego, and to the demands of the superego. This is the sense in which it seems proper to use the concept of regression. This definition emphasizes that aspect of regression previously referred to as "genetic." It stresses the importance of maturational and developmental processes in shaping the form and function of the psychic apparatus.

There are four essential features of regression which we should like to emphasize.

1. Regression is a universal tendency of mental functioning.
2. Primitive forms of mental activity are persistent and may exist side by side with more mature forms of mental functioning.
3. Many forms of regression, perhaps most, are transient and reversible.

[71]

4. As a rule regression is neither global nor uniform. It usually affects particular aspects of the instinctual life, or of ego or superego functioning, rather than the whole of either, and what functions it does affect, are affected to different degrees.

1. Regression is a universal tendency of mental functioning. Writing in 1915, Freud said,

> . . . the development of the mind shows a peculiarity which is present in no other developmental process . . . one can describe the state of affairs, which has nothing to compare with it, only by saying that in this case every earlier stage of development persists alongside the later stage which has arisen from it. . . . The earlier mental state may not have manifested itself for years, but none the less it is so far present that it may at any time again become the mode of expression of the forces in the mind, and indeed the only one, as though all later developments had been annulled or undone. This extraordinary plasticity of mental developments is not unrestricted as regards direction; it may be described as a special capacity for involution— for regression—since it may well happen that a later and higher stage of development, once abandoned, cannot be reached again. But the primitive stages can always be re-established; the primitive mind is, in the fullest meaning of the word, imperishable [1915c, p. 285f.].

This quotation from Freud constitutes a commentary on psychic functioning in general. All aspects of mental life are subject to regressive change. Anna Freud (1951, 1963) considers regression a characteristic process in the normal development of psychic structure. Piaget (1937) in his careful observations of mental development has described how regression appears in connection with each advance toward a new level of mental functioning. *The past is always a potentially active element in mental life.*

Evidence of regressive activity can be seen in every individual at some time or other. The level of operation of any mental function is subject to continuous flux reflecting the revival of primitive wishes or reactivating modes of functioning which were characteristic for the individual during the early years of his life. Regression, in fact, is one of the most characteristic qualities of the manner in which the mental apparatus works.

2. Primitive forms of mental activity are persistent and may exist side by side with more mature forms of mental functioning. Because a certain level of function has been reached it does not follow that this level will be maintained at all times. Instances of normal regressive phenomena are ubiquitous and well known. The most commonly cited example is the recurrent normal regression which takes place during sleep in the process of dreaming. There are, of course, many other forms of regression which are typical of everyday waking mental life. The magical thinking which forms part of all popular superstitions may be quoted as an example. Another example is to be found in the practically universal experience of daydreaming.

The attainment of more "mature" forms of mental functioning does not necessarily imply that the more primitive wishes or modes of functioning have disappeared. It means only that the later mental acquisitions are the more dominant. They constitute the more usual, the preferred, and the more acceptable modes of functioning. They are the ones that may be said to occupy the foreground of psychic life. The more primitive forms of functioning persist, but they are held in abeyance. They may be considered to be in the background. Nonetheless, they exist as a rule alongside the more mature forms of functioning and under appropriate circumstances they may come to dominate the operation of one or more parts of the mental apparatus. This important point will be discussed more fully below.

3. Regression is not necessarily permanent. Most regressions, especially those of ego functions, are temporary and reversible. Because of the problems we face in clinical practice, we tend to be impressed much more with the relatively stabilized expressions of regression. These regressive phenomena are seen in the symptoms and pathological character traits for which our patients consult us. They are in a sense "structured" regressions, and their impact on the observer is all the more striking since they contribute to disturbing phenomena which are outside of the realm of the ego's mastery.

On the other hand, there are many regressive phenomena which are particularly striking, precisely because they operate in the service of the ego. They are primitive tendencies which appear in pursuit of certain needs, goals, or interests of the ego. These phenomena will also be discussed more fully later in this chapter.

Under the special conditions of psychoanalytic therapy, very primitive wishes or modes of functioning may be temporarily reactivated. The same is true of the hypnagogic period. Profound regression, e.g., the Isakower (1938) phenomenon, may take place. It should be emphasized that the deep forms of regression encountered under the special circumstances just mentioned, are not in themselves ominous. The degree of regression during an analytic session does not constitute a reliable measure of the severity of the patient's psychopathology. What determines the severity of psychic illness is not the depth of regression at a particular moment, or under special circumstances, but rather its persistent, irreversible nature, the degree of conflict which it generates, and its effect upon adaptation.

4. As a rule regressions are specific and discrete in nature rather than global and total. This applies to derivatives of all the three main portions of the psychic apparatus, the id, the ego, and the superego.

It will be convenient to begin by observing the regression of id derivatives, i.e., drive regression. The manifestations of such regression are very well known because they play an important role in the formation of neurotic symptoms. At the core of each neurotic symptom is an unconscious fantasy which contains some instinctual wish of childhood. The neurotic symptom reflects the reactivation of a wish from the oral, anal, or phallic levels of the childhood instinctual organization. It should be noted, however, that only a few of the primitive expressions of the drive reappear in the regressed psychic derivatives. The unconscious fantasy behind the symptom expresses a specific, discrete, instinctual demand. A good illustration is to be seen in the vicissitudes of the anal drives. Let us take the case of an accountant whose work and personal habits reveal the typical character structure based on reaction formation against anal instinctual wishes. His choice of profession, furthermore, has been determined by a sublimation of various anal trends. Under certain conditions, he develops a neurosis characterized by obsessive-compulsive symptoms. Analysis reveals that these symptoms represent the result of inadequate defenses against a wish to kill or impregnate through the use of anal gas. The symptom is based upon a regressive reactivation of certain anal wishes of childhood. While he develops these symptoms, however, his reactive character traits remain as firm and as stable as before, and he continues his professional activity without evidence of conflict or inhibition. In addition, the normal component of the anal drives in sexual foreplay remains unaffected. What can we learn from this about the

[75]

process of instinctual regression? Clearly, when a drive undergoes regressive transformation only a small portion of its activity is involved. The entire component-drive organization is not affected. Mature forms of drive gratification, e.g., foreplay activity, may persist alongside primitive expressions of the drive, e.g., the wish to kill or impregnate with gas. In addition, the character traits and sublimations which had developed out of conflict over the anal drive may retain their (secondary) autonomy. They do not necessarily have to be drawn into the pathological, regressive tendency. To be sure, in very severe mental illness, as in schizophrenia, a very extensive regressive involvement of the drive organization may take place. Incidentally, in such cases this is usually accompanied by a correspondingly major involvement of the ego functions (cf. Chapter 8).

In contrast to the manifestations of instinctual-drive regression, much less is known in a systematic way about regression of ego functions. This is due to the historical fact that conflicts over instinctual drives were among the first pathological formations which were discovered and studied in psychoanalysis. The introduction of the structural theory, however, with its emphasis on maturation and development, has furnished a framework within which the regression of ego functions may be studied more precisely. As a result, in recent years, following the pioneer studies of Anna Freud and Hartmann, there has been a growing interest in the study of ego development. Until recently, developmental psychologists had done most of the work in this field. Now, however, psychoanalysts using long-range, longitudinal studies have begun to make their contributions to our knowledge concerning the development of ego functions. The elaboration of a detailed, sequential description of the development of the ego, from the psychoanalytic point of view, will advance immeasurably our knowledge of regressive ego phenomena.

The distinction which Hartmann (1939a, 1950b) has made between primary and secondary autonomy is of special significance in this connection. According to the topographic hypothesis, the mental apparatus can be regarded primarily as an instrument for the discharge of instinctual tensions. What we would nowadays call functions of the ego have their origin, according to the topographic theory, exclusively in the impact of a frustrating environment upon the drives. In other words, ego functions came into being as a consequence of some instinctual vicissitude. Observational data indicate that this is not always the case. Hartmann has pointed out that certain functions of the ego are autonomous from the very beginning. They are part of the native endowment of the human species and they appear inexorably in the course of maturation. There are other functions, however, which do originate as a consequence of intrapsychic conflict. The successful resolution of conflicts may result in the formation of permanent ego structures or functions which are stable in nature, which are under the control of the ego, and whose mode of activity no longer reflects the impulsive nature of the original drive component. Sublimations, character traits, and various ego interests are examples of the products of this type of resolution of psychic conflict. Such activities are considered to be secondarily autonomous.

According to the structural theory, one can postulate a progressive developmental direction of the ego functions vis-à-vis the drives. This direction is toward increasing ego autonomy, toward increasing control of the ego over derivatives of the id, increasing ability of the ego to neutralize drive cathexes and in so doing to bring these drive energies under its mastery and at its disposal as the executant of the psychic apparatus. Conversely, a movement in the opposite direction, a loss of secondary autonomy, constitutes regressive deterioration of the ego function. Such phenomena are regressive because they represent the re-emergence of more primitive modes of mental operation. The inability to distinguish sensory perceptions of the external world from fantasies, for example, or the disintegration of a sublimation into its instinctual antecedents, may be viewed as regressions of ego function.

A special form of ego mastery should be mentioned at this point, namely, the ability of the ego to intiate regression of its own functions in furtherance of its interests. Such regressions are called regressions in the service of the ego (Kris, 1934). They imply a flexibility on the part of the ego, an ability to employ at will more primitive modes of functioning. Such regressions are usually accompanied by a diminution of control over discharge of drive cathexes resulting in patterns of more rapid discharge. They can, however, be interrupted and controlled by the ego. The inability to initiate regression of this sort characterizes the obsessional personality, the obsessive-compulsive neurotic, and certain schizophrenics; it renders their treatment by psychoanalytic methods very difficult. Controlled ego regressions are essential to the enjoyment of art and humor, of play, of sexual relations, and to imagination and creative activity in general. Regressions in the service of the ego constitute regressions in a genetic sense because they revive earlier forms of ego function (see also Hartmann, 1939b).

Regression of ego functions is thus part of everyday experience. Transient ego regressions may be observed in both normal and pathological contexts. They form the basis of such phenomena as temporary disturbances in the sense of identity, transient episodes of depersonalization and derealization, *déjà vu,* and disturbances in the sense of time. Transient regressions of this type are particularly common in the course of psychoanalytic treatment.

According to Hartmann (1958), one of the most important measures of ego strength is the ability of the ego during intrapsychic conflict to resist the tendency toward regressive involvement of its stabilized, secondarily autonomous functions. All neurotic symptom formation represents a certain degree of limitation of ego control over its functions. In schizophrenia, however, a process of much graver consequence ensues. One of the characteristic features of this disturbance is weakness of the ego. This weakness becomes manifest by way of the regressive reinstinctualization of many functions which had achieved a high degree of autonomy. However, even in schizophrenia, the process of regression of ego functions is not a global one. Not all ego functions are affected with equal intensity in every case. Many ego functions remain quite uninvolved.

This latter observation has aroused certain speculations concerning the developmental course of ego functions. It seems a plausible conclusion that there may be either congenital weaknesses of certain ego functions or, more likely, that there may be weak spots in the developmental history of some of these functions. Such critical points in the development of ego function would be analogous to the more familiar fixation points of the instinctual drives. Beres (1956), following Hartmann (1950b), studied the developmental disturbances of ego functions. He demonstrated that such disturbances may be discrete. They involve specific ego functions in a selective manner. He suggested that patho-

[79]

logical object relationships and difficulties encountered in establishing normal identifications could interfere with the evolution of stable ego functions and render them vulnerable to regressive involvement. Under favorable circumstances, the untoward effects of such developmental disturbances can be overcome. In certain critical circumstances, however, a permanent impairment or loss of certain ego functions may take place. Anna Freud (1951) has shown how children will respond to crises by regression rather than by symptom formation. Adult patients of the borderline type and patients with psychoses do likewise.

The analogy between libidinal fixations and developmental weakness of the ego, both serving as points for regression, may be carried further. Libidinal regression often occurs to a level of fixation at which gratification has been intense and consistent. As regards ego functioning, Kris (1950b) and others have described regressive reactivation in conflict situations of earlier, successful modes of ego mastery. These considerations have been used as the basis for a fresh approach to the problem of the choice of neurosis. Wangh (1959) traced the developmental history of certain ego functions in a case of phobia and was able to advance certain hypotheses to explain how the interaction of ego development and instinctual conflict made the choice of phobic mechanisms an almost inevitable and predictable solution of his patient's conflicts. One feature of this choice of symptom was the regressive reactivation of successful modes of adaptation utilized earlier in life and associated with ties to gratifying libidinal objects.

Regression of superego function has been referred to earlier in this chapter in connection with delusions of self-observation. Many of the considerations which apply to the developmental direction of ego functions apply to the development of those of the superego as well. The recent literature of psychoanalysis contains many contributions which attempt to record in detailed fashion the successive phases of superego development. This development points toward the replacement of guilt by judgment, toward the replacement of automatic, affective reactions by more controlled, realistic considerations. In effect, one might paraphrase the famous dictum: "Where id was there shall ego be," to read, "Where superego was there shall ego be."

The regression of superego functions, like that of ego functions, is a selective, not a global process. The superego is not an entity. It is made up of innumerable demands, some of which are precisely related to specific situations. This becomes apparent when we reflect on our clinical experience. There are patients who feel very guilty in connection with certain situations and impulses, but who nevertheless remain relatively unmoved by other conflicts. Even if they are moved, they may feel the need for punishment in a less primitive or less drastic fashion. Delusions, fantasies, and dream material often represent in concrete and precise form the specific object relationship which is regressively expressed in the particular superego demand. Accordingly, it is not at all surprising that regression of the superego is selective and specific rather than global.

Certain characteristic features of superego functioning betray their primitive origin, for example, the regressive reactivation of the talion principle, the mechanism of undoing, and the increasingly instinctual quality of superego pressure. In addition, many regressive manifestations of the superego are derived from experiences of the prephallic phase and they involve elements of behavior which actually comprise precursors of the superego (Bak, 1939; Jacobson, 1954; Weissman, 1954).

SUMMARY

1. We have reviewed the history of the development of the concept of regression and we have observed how the meaning of this term was expanded steadily to explain different types of phenomena. We have described five different ways in which the term regression has been used: genetic, systemic, instinctual, phylogenetic, and biogenetic. We have considered the different uses of the concept regression within the framework of the structural theory and have concluded that regression in the phylogenetic and biogenetic sense is of limited use scientifically and that the concept of systemic regression is inconsistent with the structural theory.

2. Regression is defined as the re-emergence of modes of mental functioning characteristic of earlier phases of psychic development.

3. The process of regression may affect all the three portions of the psychic apparatus, the ego, the id, and the superego. Regression is a general tendency of mental life. Drive regression and ego regression may be independent variables. Drive regression by itself does not determine the ego regression.

4. Regression affects the functioning of the constituent parts of the psychic apparatus in a selective and specific fashion. Regression is not global.

5. Regressions are usually transient and reversible. Pathology is not determined by the depth of the regression but rather by its irreversible nature, by the conflict which it engenders, and by its interference with the process of adaptation.

6. Primitive modes of mental function exist side by side with more mature forms. What is observed in regressive phenomena is a shift in dominance of function. In regressive phenomena the primitive aspects of function which had been controlled and held in abeyance come to the fore.

7

The Primary and Secondary Processes

In this chapter we propose to evaluate another set of psychoanalytic concepts in the light of the transition from the topographic to the structural theory. These concepts are the primary and secondary processes.

As pointed out in Chapter 2, the assumption that there are two types of mental functioning, one called the primary process and the other the secondary process, is an integral part of the topographic theory. We wish to emphasize that this assumption is one that has to do essentially with mental energies. It constitutes one of the fundamental aspects of psychoanalysis as a dynamic psychology, a psychology which uses energic principles. Freud's purpose in dividing mental activities on the basis of whether they function according to the primary or secondary process was to offer a satisfactory explanation of what happens to the energy of an unconscious instinctual impulse from the time of its initiation in the system *Ucs.* to its final expression as a conscious mental experience. It enabled him to bring together various mental phenomena on the basis of the degree of mobility of cathexis by which each could be characterized. Such divergent phenomena as dreams, neurotic symptoms, jokes, and parapraxes could be understood to share the common feature of a high degree of mobility of cathexis. Ordinary, rational thought, on the other hand, was related to mental cathexes which were bound, or relatively immobile.

The concepts of primary and secondary process are closely related in the topographic theory to the idea of regression, specifically to systemic and genetic regression. Systemic regression implies the re-emergent dominance of the system *Ucs.*, together with a reversion to types of wishes and mental activity characteristic of the earliest periods of life. With this regression there is a shift to primary-process functioning.

The primary process is the type of mental functioning characteristic of the system *Ucs.* It is also the manner in which the mind functions during the earliest period of life before the system *Pcs.* comes into being. It is for this reason that it is called primary.[1]

The fundamental characteristic of the primary process is **the tendency** for instinctual cathexes to press for full and rapid discharge. Full discharge of cathexes results in feelings of pleasure or the cessation of feelings of unpleasure. The high degree of mobility which is the hallmark of the primary process is in keeping with the pleasure principle which holds sway in the system *Ucs.* Roughly stated, discharge equals pleasure and pleasure is the only concern of the system *Ucs.* Nothing in the system *Ucs.* impedes the tendency toward full and rapid discharge of cathexes. Any object or avenue of discharge can be used for that purpose regardless of the demands of morality or considerations of causality, logic, and

[1] Schilder (1928) considered this type of mental operation to be primary in the sense that it constitutes the beginning phases, the first steps in the transformation of an impulse into a mental representation, or the first step in the conversion of an instinctual cathexis into a dream, a joke, or a slip of the tongue.

reality. The ultimate goal of the primary-process tendency is, according to Freud, to achieve a set of perceptions which is identical with earlier sensory experiences that had been accompanied by pleasurable gratification. This has been discussed in Chapter 2. What is implied in this tendency is the notion that the achievement of such an identity of perception is the equivalent of a complete or massive discharge of drive cathexes. Other activities, such as thinking, for example, imply a lesser discharge of instinctual tension.

The clinical phenomena which illustrate the primary-process tendency are those which are characterized by the mechanisms of displacement and condensation. This type of mobility of cathexes was important in the explanation of the origin of dreams in the topographic theory which will be discussed more fully in Chapter 9.

The secondary process is the mode of functioning typical for the system *Pcs.* Like the system *Pcs.* itself, this quality of mental functioning is a later acquisition of the mind. The secondary process results from the impact of reality and of the environment upon the developing mental apparatus. It reflects the effects of experiences of mastering frustration, of being rewarded by important objects in the environment, and of socially determined moral precepts. From the energic point of view, the tendency of the secondary process is to delay, modify, tone down, or oppose the discharge of the drive cathexes. Presumably, according to the topographic theory, this is made possible by the greater energic potential of the system *Pcs.*

The fundamental characteristic of the secondary process is stability of cathexes. Secondary-process cathexes are "bound" by the process of being attached to word and object representations which are fixed and constant. A freely mobile displacement of cathexes or the condensation of many cathexes onto one mental element is not ordinarily possible. One word or object may not be substituted so readily for another, nor may a part of an object be used to represent the whole. When cathexes are bound in such a manner, when words and objects come to have fixed relationships, logic and causality become possible. Thus the laws of syntax, freedom from contradiction, and realistic temporal relations become part of secondary-process activity. The binding of drive cathexes to fixed word and object representations is an essential step in the development of the reality principle. It serves the end of making it possible to achieve realistic gratification and thus becomes an important element in the process of adaptation.

Thus we can see that according to the topographic theory, there are two fundamentally different types of mental activity. Mental activity in the system *Ucs.* is characterized by mobile cathexes and follows the laws of the primary process. Mental activity in the systems *Pcs.* and *Cs.* is characterized by bound cathexes and follows the laws of the secondary process.

Considerable obscurity and confusion have surrounded the concept of the primary process. It is perhaps one of the most difficult of psychoanalytic ideas to grasp. The reasons for this confusion are not hard to find. The term has been employed in many ways. Freud himself used the concept of primary process in the sense just given. In the literature of psychoanalysis, however, the term primary process has often been used as synonymous with irrational or unrealistic thought or fantasy. It has come to mean unconscious mental activity in general. By the same token the term secondary process has been used to mean ordinary rational thinking, instead of being used, as Freud used it, to refer to the binding of cathexes. It is the binding of cathexes (the secondary process) which makes rational thought and realistic action

[87]

possible, according to the topographic theory, just as it is the mobility of cathexes (primary process) which leads to condensation and displacement.

We may now turn to a consideration of the problems involved in transferring the terms primary and secondary process to the conceptual framework of the structural theory. We have already noted (Chapters 4 and 5) that the accumulation of new clinical data between 1900 and 1920 induced Freud to alter the topographic theory in certain fundamental respects and to substitute for it what we call the structural theory. Are these new data consistent with the concepts of a primary and a secondary process of mental functioning as Freud formulated them in 1900? We have already emphasized that these two concepts were of basic importance in the topographic theory. Do they also require some revision in order to be consonant with the rest of the structural theory, or can they be carried over unchanged, as is sometimes assumed? If revision is necessary, how much is required and what must it be?

Let us begin by taking note of Freud's discussion of this problem. In *The Interpretation of Dreams* (1900) he stated that the system *Ucs.* is composed solely of freely mobile cathexes seeking discharge. The system *Pcs.*, on the other hand, has definite, fixed, and stable representations for words and objects. Fifteen years later, in his paper on "The Unconscious" (1915b) Freud took cognizance of certain difficulties in this point of view. The stumbling block was to be found in the existence of repressed, unconscious fantasies. Because they are not readily accessible to consciousness and because they produce derivatives which indicate the impulsiveness of their nature and the mobility of their cathexes, such fantasies, in the topographic hypothesis, should be considered portions of the system *Ucs.* On the other hand, because

[88]

such fantasies are made up of definite verbal concepts and object representations and because they demonstrate features of the secondary process, such fantasies should be considered part of the system *Pcs.* Freud wrote:

> Among the derivatives of the *Ucs.* instinctual impulses . . . there are some which unite in themselves characters of an opposite kind. On the one hand, they are highly organized, free from self-contradiction, have made use of every acquisition of the system *Cs.* and would hardly be distinguished by our ordinary judgement from the formations of that system. On the other hand they are unconscious and incapable of becoming conscious. Thus *qualitatively* they belong to the system *Pcs.,* but *factually* to the *Ucs.* . . . Of such a nature are those phantasies of normal people as well as of neurotics which we have recognized as preliminary stages in the formation both of dreams and of symptoms and which, in spite of their high degree of organization, remain repressed and therefore cannot become conscious. . . . Substitutive formations, too, are highly organized derivatives of the *Ucs.* of this kind; but these succeed in breaking through into consciousness, when circumstances are favourable—for example, if they happen to join forces with an anticathexis from the *Pcs.* [1915b, p. 190f.].

[Further in the same essay, Freud wrote:] The reason for all these difficulties is to be found in the circumstance that the attribute of being conscious, which is the only characteristic of psychical processes that is directly presented to us, is in no way suited to serve as a criterion for the differentiation of systems. Apart from the fact that the conscious is not always conscious but also at times latent, observation has shown that much that shares the characteristics of the system *Pcs.* does not become conscious; . . . Hence consciousness stands in no simple relation either to the different systems or to repression. The truth is that it is not only the psychically repressed that remains alien to consciousness, but also some of the

[89]

impulses which dominate our ego—something, therefore, that forms the strongest functional antithesis to the repressed [p. 192].

We see from these quotations that as early as 1915, Freud recognized that secondary-process phenomena may be associated with elements of the system *Ucs.* In other words, the simple statement that the system *Ucs.* operates according to the primary process and the system *Pcs.* operates according to the secondary process required modification. The dichotomy —*Ucs.*-primary process, *Pcs.*-secondary process—a fundamental feature of the topographic theory, does not hold up. The awareness of this contradiction within the topographic theory was one of the factors which stimulated Freud to study the possibility for instituting a new frame of reference for psychoanalysis. The structural theory was the outcome of this study.

How then should the terms primary process and secondary process be understood within the framework of the structural hypothesis? Primary process, we suggest, should be used to refer to mobility of instinctual cathexes and their tendency to rapid discharge. This was Freud's original formulation of the concept. Mobility of cathexes becomes manifest pre-eminently in those phenomena which demonstrate the effect of displacement and condensation of drive cathexes. Examples of high degrees of cathectic mobility are readily available in the analysis of dreams. It is this quality which accounts for the absurdities and contradictions which one finds in dreams. When cathectic energies are easily shifted from realistically appropriate objects to inappropriate ones, causal relationships and logic and temporal sequences are inevitably overthrown. The effect is that of complete disregard for reality. Strictly speaking, the characteristics just mentioned are the end results of mobility of cathexes. They are the effects of the primary process, not the primary process itself, as noted earlier.

If we utilize this definition of the primary process within the framework of the structural theory, we should make the following points which are basic. Each one of the points will be discussed at greater length in the remaining portion of this chapter.

1. The activities of the ego and superego as well as those of the id may be characterized by the primary process.

2. Primary-process tendencies remain active throughout life. Mature mental functioning does not imply a complete suppression or cessation of such activity.

3. Primary-process phenomena are not necessarily pathological, nor are they always maladaptive.

4. No sharp line of distinction can be drawn between those phenomena in which cathexes are firmly bound (secondary process) and those phenomena in which cathexes are highly mobile (primary process). There is instead a continuum of phenomena which demonstrate varying degrees of mobility of cathexis. The difference between primary and secondary process is actually a quantitative one indicating the degree of mobility of cathexes. It reflects the growing ability of the ego to regulate cathectic discharge.

5. Primary and secondary processes are not identical with thinking. Mobility of cathexes is a broader concept which is intended to encompass other phenomena in addition to thinking. At any moment thinking may be characterized by a greater or lesser component of mobile cathexes (primary process).

6. The close association between timelessness and primary process should be re-examined.

Let us consider each one of these points seriatim:

1. The first point in our list stated that primary-process

functioning is a tendency of mental life in general. It may characterize the activity of the superego and the ego as well as the id. The special connection between rapid mobility of cathexes and the functioning of the id is well known and has been commented upon repeatedly. No illustration of this fact need be presented here. Certain observations, however, concerning the superego and the ego are in order.

That superego function may show the hallmark of the primary process should come as no surprise. The energic investment of the superego is instinctual. Its drive endowment is primarily aggressive. Freud (1923a) noted, accordingly, that the superego in many respects is closer to the id than it is to the ego. By this he referred to the fact that the superego's demands for self-punishment may press upon the ego as urgently, as insistently, and as irrationally as any libidinal wish of the id. The self-destructive and self-punitive tendencies observed in patients suffering from psychotic depressions illustrate this statement.

There is, however, less dramatic, but equally impressive evidence of the fact that the functions of the superego may show the effects of high mobility of cathexes. Eidelberg (1936, 1944) pointed this out in connection with the analysis of parapraxes, especially certain slips of the tongue. Many slips of the tongue are based upon the break-through into speech of elements which betray the speaker, elements which expose him to shame, humiliation, and even defeat. Slips of this kind often constitute unintended confessions of guilt. They serve the interests of the superego. Like other parapraxes their mechanism is dependent on a high degree of mobility of cathexes. This mobility is manifested in the mechanisms of displacement and condensation, so typical of the primary mode of mental functioning. Examples of *ego* activities which function according to the primary process will be given later.

2. There is, of course, nothing new in the statement that primary-process tendencies remain active throughout life. In the context of the *topographic* hypothesis, however, the appearance of phenomena characterized by a high degree of cathectic mobility signifies the break-through into conscious mental functioning of elements of the system *Ucs.* It indicates an irruption of repressed, archaic, libidinal, childhood wishes which disregard reality and which are maladaptive or comical in their effects. As mentioned earlier in this volume, this formulation is in conflict with many facts of clinical experience. The structural hypothesis offers a framework which is free of these contradictions.

During the earliest phases of life the psychic apparatus functions according to the primary process; that is to say, its activity is characterized by a very high degree of cathectic mobility. This may be recognized in the tendency toward immediate or very rapid discharge of drive cathexes. From the outset, therefore, the psychic apparatus is under the complete domination of the pleasure principle.

With the development of the ego, however, this situation begins to change. According to Anna Freud (1936), the core of the ego as an organized system may be said to reside in its role of inhibiting or suppressing the discharge of instinctual cathexes. As stated in the previous chapter, one can postulate a general tendency in the direction of an increasing capacity of the ego to master the discharge of drive cathexes. This mastery, however, does not always take the form of suppression or opposition. As executant of the psychic apparatus the ego facilitates and makes possible drive discharge. It does so with due regard for demands of reality and the superego. In addition, the ego "tames" or "neutralizes" drive energy for its own purposes (Hartmann, 1939a, 1950b). Some ego functions, however, may be carried out with unneutralized drive energy. Kris (1934) has called attention to a very important group of ego functions which have in common the initiation by the ego of regressive mental functioning. Essentially, these are phenomena in which more primitive patterns of mental activity emerge. They are activities which are characterized by high cathectic mobility, yet they emerge in a context which could hardly be considered pathological. Thus we can see that mental activity according to the primary process is characteristic not only of early childhood and of pathological phenomena but also of adult ego activities which may be normal and adaptive.

3. The fact that primary-process phenomena are not necessarily pathological and that they are not always maladaptive follows quite logically from the considerations mentioned in the preceding paragraph. The literature of psychoanalysis which deals with creative thinking, scientific discovery, and artistic experiences is replete with examples in which new insights and realistic advances resulted from mental activity which was characterized by a high degree of mobility of the cathectic investment of mental representations. Play activity, the enjoyment of art, and psychoanalytic therapy are other examples of activities in which primary process may characterize an adaptive activity. If we follow the structural hypothesis consistently, we can see that it is not the influence of unconscious mental activity alone, nor the fact that its energic investment is very mobile, which determines whether or not an activity is pathological.

4. According to the structural theory and the principle of multiple function, any mental activity represents the result of the integration by the ego of the demands of the various agencies of the mind. In addition, the ego takes into

account the individual's relationship to reality. A wide and varied range of mental activities may result from this integrative effort. These activities demonstrate many different patterns of cathectic mobility. In some instances one may observe a high degree of cathectic mobility, in other instances the opposite may be the case. In between is a broad spectrum of activities or functions which demonstrate varying degrees of cathectic mobility. Artistic creativity is of course one of the richest areas from which examples may be drawn to illustrate this point. Some artistic sublimations are carried out in a controlled, neutral fashion indicating a high level of ego mastery. They depend upon stable patterns of cathectic discharge. Other equally successful artistic activities are carried out in a manner which makes it appear that the ego has been overwhelmed. The artist experiences the creative urge in a passive manner (Kris, 1939), flooded by a plethora of impressions, thoughts, and images. In such cases ego control is intact even though the regression of function may have been considerable and the patterns of cathectic discharge very rapid.

The following clinical fragment (Arlow, 1952) illustrates a sublimation which was carried out under conditions of rapid cathectic discharge. Although clearly dependent upon primary-process functioning, the sublimation of the instinctual energies involved was both realistic and adaptive. This material is from the analysis of a young married woman suffering from hysteria. She was frigid. The analytic material revealed that she had the idea that without a penis orgasm is impossible. Her unconscious conflict centered about her wish to possess by force and to enjoy the use of her father's penis. Her father was a very successful and powerful man. He had done brilliantly in his own profession, in hobbies, in sports, and in various business ventures. The patient had considerable artistic talent. During the analysis she began to devote this talent to the decoration of her new home. Unconsciously her house represented her body, and decorating it had the significance of correcting the ugliness of being without a penis. Her concern over furnishing and decorating her house was soon drawn into the unconscious conflict over the wish to seize her father's phallus. At every phase of the decorating of her house she wanted to obtain from her father money, furniture, wood, or some other item which she could use to adorn her home. In the midst of one such experience, she reported the following episode:

She was sitting in bed one morning sipping coffee and smoking a cigarette. She was thinking of how to furnish one of the rooms. She decided she needed a certain kind of desk but could not afford it. "Perhaps," she thought, "my father would give me one if I were to ask him. Better yet, I'll make one myself. But I have no wood. I could ask my father for some wood, but he has used all the cherry wood in his own home." She dismissed the thought of turning to her father.

At this point she felt her thoughts coming with increasing speed and intensity; they seemed to be rapidly getting out of control. All sorts of ideas flooded in on her. She thought of various ways of combining wood, plastic, iron, and other materials to make the desk she desired. By this time the tempo of her thoughts was so rapid that she seemed to have no control over them. She was seized by a sense of overwhelming excitement. At the apex of these feelings, according to the patient, "Suddenly I got the idea that it would be possible to reconvert an old double wardrobe into a desk. The idea just clicked. It flooded me like a tremendous burst from within. When the thought reached my mind and I saw that this was it, I lost all control. I began to scream my husband's name at the top of my voice. I screamed it again and again. They [husband and the children] came running into the room. From the way I was screaming they thought something had happened, something was wrong. I could not control it. I kept shouting, 'I have it, I have it!' As soon as I saw them I began to babble away a mile a minute how I was going to redesign the desk, how I would arrange the drawers, how much it would cost, where I would put it, etc. I couldn't stop talking. I was getting more and more out of breath. Finally the excitement seemed to wear off, almost suddenly. The tension left me. I felt relaxed. I felt all in. I was tired. I was completely spent."

In relating this experience during the session, the patient realized what she had not been aware of at the time of the experience, namely, that the mounting crescendo, the creative idea coming at the apex of excitement, and the uncontrollable outpouring of feeling with a subsequent relaxation and desire to sleep all recapitulated the sequence of events in an orgasm. The patient had a creative spell which simulated orgasm. She was not at all conscious of any sexual feeling. This is an example of an ego activity—artistic creation—being carried out successfully and consciously according to the pattern of primary-process discharge.

5. What is the relationship of primary process, as defined in this chapter, to thinking? In the light of what has been said so far it should be clear that in the framework of the structural theory, the primary process is not considered as a form of thinking. It is a mental process which is involved in some instances of thinking. If we are consistent in our terminology and if we define the primary process in terms of high mobility of cathexes, we must conclude that the concept of the primary process is broader than thinking. Thinking is an ego function, partly autonomous in origin and richly

influenced by the vicissitudes of the drives. Thinking, like other ego functions, e.g., perception, may become a vehicle for drive discharge. Under such circumstances its functioning may be characterized by varying degrees of cathectic mobility depending upon the interaction of forces in the ego as described earlier. Thinking characterized by highly mobile cathexes need not be unrealistic or maladaptive. Whether it is or not depends very much on the element of ego control. On the contrary, the ability to give free reign to primary-process tendencies often plays an important adaptive role in thinking which is used in problem solving and scientific creativeness. Conversely, the inability to give free reign to primary-process tendencies in thinking may, under certain circumstances, be maladaptive. Such an inability may interfere with certain types of work, play, and with psychoanalytic treatment.

Since rapid cathectic discharge is not always pathological, its juxtaposition and opposition to the concept of secondary-process thinking as rational, adaptive, and reality oriented, a concept inherited from the topographic theory, is no longer significant. It would seem advantageous to conceptualization in psychoanalysis if one dropped the term "secondary process" when it is used synonymously with conscious thinking and simply referred to thinking as thinking.

Functions of the ego, other than thinking, may be involved in rapid cathectic discharge and operate according to the primary process. This consideration has a bearing on hallucinations and dreams (see Chapter 9). A few observations concerning the function of perception and its relation to mobility of cathexes will be discussed now.

Ordinarily, perception is regarded as an autonomous ego function. Under certain conditions, however, and for relatively brief periods, the function of perception may become

[98]

a vehicle for the discharge of drive cathexes and accordingly may operate under the influence of highly mobile cathexes. Part of what is considered the sensitivity of the artist may be ascribed to this phenomenon. His perception of the external world is often fraught with the potential for rapid, mobile discharge of drive cathexes. This tendency is present in all individuals in varying degrees. Study of the conditions under which one experiences illusions or distortions of reality like *déjà vu* or distortions of time sense (Arlow, 1959) demonstrates how tensions from the drives may utilize the data of perception in order to effect rapid cathectic discharge.

It may be noted in passing that one element seems specially significant in such situations. This is the element of ambiguity (Kris and Kaplan, 1952). When the data of perception are ambiguous, i.e., when their form as perceived does not correspond readily to fixed and familiar concepts, the pressure from the drives and the defensive needs of the ego may use such percepts more readily for rapid cathectic discharge. Kris emphasized the importance of this element in the aesthetic experience. Apparently this element is basic also in understanding the reactions to Rorschach images. The element of ambiguity may be responsible for the facility with which certain phenomena of a primary-process nature appear in the experiments with the tachistoscope (Fisher, 1957).

6. In the topographic theory disturbances in the sense of time have been described as characteristic of the system *Ucs.* and the primary process. This idea stems from two sources in that theory. First it stems from the fact that one of the striking characteristics of dreams is the complete disregard of temporal relations. The statement has been made that in the system *Ucs.*, where the primary process reigns supreme, there is no sense of time. The second source of the notion of the timelessness of the primary process derives from the

fact that during treatment, in analyzing the wishes behind dreams, symptoms, and other mental products, one keeps encountering in their pristine form, vital and unchanged, the long-forgotten wishes of childhood. Since the evidence for the existence of these wishes becomes manifest during treatment in association with phenomena which demonstrate primary-process tendencies, the notion of the timelessness of the system *Ucs.* developed. Loewenstein (1958) has reported the contents of his correspondence with Freud concerning the concept of the timelessness of the system *Ucs.* In response to Loewenstein's criticism, Freud answered that he intended this expression to relate only to the fact that unconscious wishes persist and remain active until they are made conscious, at which time through the process of association and reality testing they can be correlated with reality.

According to the structural theory, the conceptualization of time depends upon the maturation and development of the ego during childhood. For the first several years of life the child has no concept of time or an inadequate one. Those phenomena (dreams, symptoms) which in a large measure derive from infantile sources often reflect the little child's inadequate or absent sense of time.

Clinical distortions of the sense of time are not directly related to primary-process mobility of cathexis. Such feelings as time seeming to stand still or that a very long period seemed to have been lived through in what was actually a very short space of time, the feeling that one is a child again, the feeling of having experienced a particular situation at an earlier time, etc., are phenomena which results from intrapsychic conflict. They are related to specific fantasies in which ideas involving time play an important part. They are not simply a direct consequence of primary-process mobility of cathexis. This point may be illustrated in the following clinical examples (Arlow, 1957).

On the Monday following Father's Day, a young woman patient began her session by stating that she felt 100 years had passed since the previous session on Friday. Her association to this statement led to the fairy tale "Sleeping Beauty." The patient concentrated on two themes. First, that all the occupants of the palace had not died but had only been asleep for 100 years. Second, that the prince who awakened her belonged to another generation. He had not yet been born at the time when the princess fell under the magical spell. Further associations concerned her being glad to see the analyst after the week end and longings for her dead father. This patient felt guilty because she blamed herself for her father's untimely death. The "Sleeping Beauty" fairy tale contained elements which corresponded to several important wishes of the patient, a self-punitive wish to change places with her father, a wish to be reunited with him, a wish to bring him back to life, and finally a typical oedipal wish of breaching the time and incest barrier by marrying someone of another generation. Her temporarily distorted sense of time was connected with the fantasy of being the sleeping beauty.

Another patient reported the following experience which took place when his mother's death from cancer was imminent. He kept waking up early in the morning long before his customary time for rising. Each time he looked at the clock and reached the reassuring conclusion that he could return safely to sleep, there was still lots of time. In his associations he revealed that he had a fantasy of magically extending the duration of each minute in order to prolong his mother's life or, more accurately, to delay the moment of her death.

SUMMARY

In this section we have made the following points:

1. The concepts of primary and secondary process should be defined in terms of varying degrees of mobility of cathexes. There is a continuum of phenomena demonstrating more or less mobility of cathexes.

2. The regulation of cathectic discharge is a function of the ego. This function may be affected by many factors.

3. No sharp line of demarcation can be drawn between primary- and secondary-process phenomena.

4. Phenomena characterized by rapid cathectic discharge are not necessarily pathological, nor are they always maladaptive. Regressions in the service of the ego constitute important illustrations of this thesis.

5. Patterns of rapid discharge of cathexes may mark the operations of the id, ego, and superego.

6. Primary and secondary processes are not identical with thinking.

7. Functions other than thinking, dreaming, and symptom formation may become involved in patterns of high cathectic mobility.

8. The concept of time appears only gradually in the course of the maturation of the growing child's ego functions. Clinical disturbances of the sense of time result from intrapsychic conflict. They are related to fantasies in which ideas about time play an important part. They are not simply a consequence of primary-process mobility of cathexes.

8

The Place of the Concepts *"Preconscious"* and *"Unconscious"* in the Structural Theory

W<small>HEN</small> F<small>REUD</small> introduced the structural theory in 1923 he suggested that the terms unconscious and preconscious should henceforth be used only in a qualitative or descriptive sense. He proposed that a distinct separation be made between the phenomenological meanings of these terms and their systemic meanings. The systemic meanings were to be dropped because they were inconsistent with his new views of the mental apparatus, which took the form of the structural theory.

In this chapter we propose to examine three points connected with the statements made in the preceding paragraph.

1. The meaning of the terms unconscious and preconscious in the topographic and structural theory.
2. How the terms unconscious and preconscious are used currently in psychoanalysis.
3. Suggestions concerning the proper place of these terms in the structural theory.

[103]

THE MEANING OF THE TERMS UNCONSCIOUS AND PRECONSCIOUS IN THE TOPOGRAPHIC AND STRUCTURAL THEORY[1]

As mentioned above, the terms unconscious and preconscious may be understood in two ways, phenomenologically and systemically. Since psychoanalysis was for a long time described as the "psychology of the unconscious," let us begin by considering the term "unconscious." Strictly speaking, from the phenomenological point of view, any mental element which is not in consciousness at a particular moment may be considered to be outside of consciousness, i.e., unconscious. Psychoanalytically, however, the term unconscious has a more precise meaning. It refers not only to the fact that certain elements may not be in consciousness at a particular moment; it means, in addition, that such elements are not accessible to consciousness or that they are accessible to consciousness only with difficulty. In order to make such elements conscious a certain amount of work has to be done. It is necessary to overcome a resistance within the mind, a resistance which is attributed to the operation of the mechanism of repression. Accordingly, if we follow the psychoanalytic use of the term unconscious, a usage which was first introduced in connection with the topographic theory, we see that mental elements which are not conscious are divisible into two groups: (a) unconscious elements, referring to those elements which are inaccessible to consciousness and which can be made accessible only with difficulty; and (2) preconscious elements, those elements which, though not conscious at the moment, are readily accessible to consciousness by the simple act of attention.

[1] The most recent extensive discussion of this matter is contained in Gill (1963). See also Eissler (1962).

In the topographic theory, moreover, when a mental element is called unconscious or preconscious certain implications of a *systemic* nature follows. We have reviewed what these systemic implications are (Chapter 2) and the reasons why Freud eventually introduced the structural theory (Chapter 4). In the latter theory, the quality of accessibility to consciousness no longer carries explicit *systemic* implications. Although Freud considered id functioning to be exclusively inaccessible to consciousness, ego functioning may be either the one or the other. Therefore, the fact that a mental element is or is not readily accessible to consciousness does not of necessity bear a particular relationship to its role in conflict, to its alignment with instinctual or anti-instinctual forces, to the nature and quality of its energic investment, or to the stage of mental development from which it has been derived. To repeat, in the structural theory the quality of accessibility to consciousness has no systemic implications.

HOW THE TERMS UNCONSCIOUS AND PRECONSCIOUS ARE USED CURRENTLY IN PSYCHOANALYSIS

The difficulties which were noted earlier over using the concepts regression and primary process without revision in both the topographic and structural frames of reference apply as well to the term preconscious. In addition, we will cite a few illustrations of the confusion which has resulted from the different uses of the term preconscious. The main point of this chapter will be to emphasize the disadvantages which follow when the term preconscious is used in an imprecise, anachronistic, and hence often in a confusing way. One can find evidence of such usage of the term preconscious in discussions of both clinical material and theory. We will begin by illustrating certain difficulties which arise in the theory of technique and therefore in actual clinical practice when the term preconscious is used in an ambiguous way.

Even among authors who have attempted to integrate the structural theory into their clinical work in a systematic fashion, one may observe how they unwittingly revert to conceptualizing in terms of the topographic theory when using the concept preconscious. Let us consider, for example, the well-known technical aphorism (Fenichel, 1939) that the proper time to interpret an unconscious wish is when preconscious derivatives appear in the analytic material. This is a conceptualization which is firmly rooted in the concept *Pcs.* as a system rather than preconscious as a quality of mental functioning. Actually, however, when derivatives of an unconscious impulse appear in the clinical material, they are conscious. The unconscious element is *inferred* from the data of consciousness. It is *not* something of which the patient can become aware by directing his attention to it. The technical aphorism quoted above therefore not only is phenomenologically inaccurate but encourages the therapist to think of conflict in terms of conscious versus unconscious and to direct his therapeutic efforts exclusively toward translating unconscious contents into consciousness. This type of procedure not only runs counter to our appreciation of the complexities of factors in conflict; it may also have very untoward consequences, especially in the treatment of children and of borderline patients. The technical rule quoted would be a good maxim to follow if repression were the only defense instituted by the ego against emergence of unconscious wishes. However, in situations where the defensive mechanisms of isolation, projection, and denial are used, elements appear in consciousness which are, nevertheless, being fended off very vigorously by the ego. A premature interpretation of such elements may be either harmful or ineffective. The following clinical experience illustrates this principle.

A young married woman came to treatment because of severe marital discord. By her impulsive and unrestrained behavior she precipitated situation after situation which eventuated in her own suffering and defeat. During the early weeks of treatment she had mentioned that her father died as the result of an automobile accident. In the third month of the analysis, however, in connection with a dream in which the corpse of a murdered man fell out of her closet, the patient gave fuller details of her father's death. The circumstances were such that the patient could be blamed in part for initiating the train of events which led to the automobile accident. As a matter of fact, the patient's mother greeted the patient shortly after the news of the father's death reached home with the accusation, "You killed him." This accusation the patient refuted with anger and she repeated her attitude of angry refutation when relating the incident in the analytic session. Thus one can see that the patient's unconscious need for punishment, connected with the idea that she was in fact responsible for her father's death, was part of the latent content of the dream. It produced derivatives which, according to the topographic theory, would be considered preconscious. Nonetheless, it would have been ineffective and perhaps even dangerous to interpret to the patient so early in her analysis that she did in fact feel that she was responsible for her father's death.

In Chapter 5 we pointed out the differences between the therapeutic task as seen from the topographic versus the structural point of view. The fact that an unconscious impulse may be inferred from the patient's conscious associations, we know today, is not the sole indication for interpreting the material. Proper technical procedure demands that an adequate assessment be made of the total relationship of the forces in conflict, an assessment which takes into account the specific forms of the patient's anxieties and the nature of the defenses which he uses to cope with them. Used in the context of the theory of technique, preconscious is vague and misleading. It often conveys the mistaken impression that the appearance in consciousness of derivatives of repressed impulses necessarily indicates a balance of forces between impulse and defense which is propitious for interpretation. This is by no means always the case.

The following clinical material is presented in order to illustrate that in giving an interpretation it is necessary to assess the total relationship of forces in the mind; one cannot be guided alone by the fact that derivatives of an unconscious wish have become manifest.

This example[2] is taken from the analysis of a thirty-year-old woman who was bitterly resentful of the fact that her father on his death had left his entire estate to his widow (the patient's mother) so that her own status had suddenly changed from that of a wealthy, protected young lady to that of a poor, self-supporting one. She now had to seek treatment for her neurosis in a clinic and to live on unemployment insurance for many weeks at a time. She had feelings of abandonment, longing, and jealous rage which were intolerable to her. She defended herself against their emergence in a variety of ways, prominent among which were isolation, denial, rationalization, and indifference.

One day, after many months of persistent analysis of her defenses, and just after she had been given notice on her job, she brought in a dream in which her mother served her two brothers, both older than herself, with food before serving

_____
[2] We are indebted to Dr. J. A. Ennis for the clinical material which follows.

the patient. During that analytic session, the last before the week end, she was able to admit that she did feel that her mother neglected her, and that she felt like the matchgirl in Andersen's story. We may say, therefore, that the months of analysis of her defenses, i.e., of demonstrating to her how she defended herself against her intolerable feelings of abandonment, longing, and rage, had produced a definite result: she could recognize the presence of such feelings on the Friday in question. Even though her defenses against them were still considerable, they were less than usual. By Monday, however, the situation had changed. On that day the patient began her session by mentioning casually that a friend had suggested that the patient sue her mother for a share of her dead father's estate. When questioned about this she described the legal basis for such a suit. She made it clear that of course this was only her friend's idea, that she herself wouldn't dream of doing such a thing, money didn't mean that much to her, and that anyway she felt very kindly toward her mother now because mother had showed that she cared about her by having called her several times over the week end, etc.

In this example the patient's desire to revenge herself on her mother as well as to force her father to prefer her to her mother and brothers was represented in consciousness at the beginning of her analytic session on Monday by a readily recognizable derivative: the idea of suing mother for a share of father's money.

This wish for vengeance clearly was not the item to interpret on that Monday morning. From the technical point of view, it is plain that the defenses against the patient's intolerably painful emotions represented the aspect of mental functioning to which the analytic work had to be directed. The patient's usual defenses of isolation, denial, rationalization, and projection had not been successful in barring from consciousness a relatively undistorted derivative of her wish for vengeance. In spite of this, however, one can see from the clinical material how her defenses were back in force after the temporary diminution of their effectiveness which had been so apparent in the previous session. These defenses and not the wish for revenge took priority in the analysis.

In other words, in a case like this where "conscious'" is not equivalent to "not strongly countercathected," we realize that we must be guided by criteria for interpretation other than the appearance of instinctual derivatives in consciousness. It is the intensity of the defensive countercathexis against the psychic element in question which is important. We know from experience that only when a defense is less intense is there a good chance that an interpretation to the patient of what it is that he is defending himself against can be assimilated or integrated with the normal or healthy part of the patient's ego.

Another type of difficulty is the following. The ambiguity which results from using the term preconscious in a phenomenological and a systemic sense at the same time, has resulted in confusion and inaccuracy in psychoanalytic writings. One can cite instances in which the term preconscious has been used to designate functions of the ego which are carried out unconsciously, and which have no relationship to the term preconscious in either of the two senses mentioned previously. For example, the phenomenon of sensory, perceptual registration outside of consciousness was first labeled preconscious perception (Fisher, 1954), despite the fact that percepts of this nature cannot be brought into consciousness by directing attention to them and that a very careful experimental procedure has to be pursued to bring them to light (Fisher and Paul, 1959, p. 72f.). This procedure affords certain data from which an inference can be made concerning the registration of the percepts. The subject of the experiment remains at all times quite unaware of the fact that certain percepts had registered in his mind. To call such phenomena preconscious can only lead to misunderstanding.

In other instances, unconscious mental operations involving problem solving, integrative thinking, or creativity have been referred to as preconscious (Kris, 1950a). Sometimes such mental activity can be made accessible to consciousness by directing attention to it; on other occasions, however, the existence of such ego operations can only be inferred. From the phenomenological point of view they are unconscious, not preconscious. The justification for labeling them preconscious derives from the posthumously published and unfinished *Outline of Psychoanalysis* (1940). In that work Freud reverted to an economic definition of preconscious which was essentially a repetition of the systemic meaning of the term in the framework of the abandoned topographic theory: a preconscious mental element is one that is cathected with bound energy, functions according to the secondary process, and belongs to the ego. It must be noted that this is a step backward from the position which Freud took in his published work from 1923 onward, namely, that preconscious should be used in a purely phenomenological sense within the framework of the structural theory. It reverts to the *systemic* meaning of the term preconscious which was characteristic of the topographic theory. It also reverts to the topographic theory's idea that the primary and secondary processes are qualitatively distinct from each other and that each characterizes the operations of a separate division of the mental apparatus (see Chapter 7).

What Freud himself would have done with this page of the *Outline* had he lived, no one can be sure. It is clear that those who follow this line of reasoning will be led in fact to attempt to combine mutually incompatible concepts of the topographic and the structural theories. They will tend to equate id with the system *Ucs.*, and ego with the system *Pcs.* with all the attendant disadvantages we have so frequently stressed.

SUGGESTIONS CONCERNING THE PROPER PLACE OF THESE TERMS IN THE STRUCTURAL THEORY

We have just described the ambiguity and confusion which attend current usage of the term preconscious. What can one suggest to improve the situation?

Even as a strictly phenomenological term which designates nothing more than the fact that a mental element not presently in consciousness can be made conscious by directing attention to it, the term preconscious is of very little value for the following reasons. In the structural theory, the importance of intrapsychic conflict in mental life is of paramount significance. As a theory it emphasizes that what we want to know concerning any particular mental element or function is its role in conflict or its relationship to conflict. Is it being defended against or is it on the side of the defenses? Is it perhaps removed from conflict altogether and thus autonomous, if an ego function, or an acceptable striving, if instinctual? These are the questions that concern us in our work as analysts. To characterize a mental element as accessible or inaccessible to consciousness does not tell us what we need to know to answer such questions. It does not tell us whether or not the mental element in which we are interested is involved in conflict. Neither does it tell us on which side of a conflict the mental element in question is to be found, i.e., whether it is allied with an instinctual derivative (a wish), with a defense, or with a self-punitive trend. When isolation, denial, and projection are used, the elements which are being defended against can enter consciousness. The fact that a mental element is preconscious in the phenomenological sense does not indicate how well it is being fended off or how significant is its role in intrapsychic conflict. The conclusion seems inevitable that the term preconscious carries such a burden of disadvantage that its use could very well be dispensed with in the structural theory. The term unconscious, on other hand, should be used to indicate that something is not conscious, whether or not it can readily become conscious.

These suggestions may seem radical to many analysts. However, they follow the idea that the terminology of a psychological theory should be consonant with its basic orientation. The words which we use in our scientific work should refer to concepts which are consistent and significant. At best the term preconscious is of little value in the structural theory, at worst it is confusing. If we are to be consistent, we should drop the term preconscious and should use the term unconscious to indicate only that something is not conscious. If we do this, our terminology will conform more closely to the principles of the structural theory and will be more useful in a practical way. Clarifying terminology and concepts is advantageous for clinical work as well as for theoretical exposition. It is a useful step in facilitating further advances in both theory and technique.

9

Dreams and the Structural Theory

LET US PAUSE a moment to review what we have done so far. After differentiating between the structural and the topographic theories of the mental apparatus, we have summarized the principal elements of each. We then compared and contrasted them, concluding that the two are distinctly different theories despite their many similarities. We pointed out, moreover, that the two theories are incompatible in the crucially important area of intrapsychic conflict, and that the superiorities of the structural theory over the topographic one require that the latter be discarded *as a theory* in favor of the former. We have gone on then to suggest refinements and redefinitions of certain concepts, still important in our theoretical framework, which were introduced by Freud long before he wrote *The Ego and the Id*. The concepts we discussed in this way are regression, the primary and secondary processes, and the concepts "unconscious" and "preconscious." In all of the foregoing discussion we have referred repeatedly to the practical, clinical importance of the theoretical issues involved. Nevertheless our principal focus has been on the understanding of theories and of theoretical concepts.

We wish now to apply our conclusions to two phenomena of great clinical importance, dreams and psychoses. We hope to show that it is not only useful, but indeed necessary to apply the explanatory concepts of the structural theory if one is to achieve a satisfactory understanding of either of these two important phenomena of mental life. In this chapter we shall attempt to demonstrate the correctness of this assertion with respect to the psychology of dreaming. In the next chapter we shall discuss the psychopathology of the psychoses.

It should be noted that this is not the prevalent opinion among analysts as far as dreams are concerned. Indeed a conviction to the contrary is rather the rule. It seems fair to say that most analysts would maintain (1) that the topographic theory is admirably adapted to an explanation of the psychology of dreaming; (2) that it is clearly superior to the structural theory in this area; and (3) that even if there were no other reason for retaining the topographic theory as a part of psychoanalytic theory, it would be necessary to retain it in order to explain the phenomena of dreams.

We shall divide the present chapter into three sections for the sake of convenience. The first section is devoted to a summary of the theory of dreaming according to the topographic theory. The second section contains a theory of dreaming within the framework of the structural theory. In the third section we shall attempt to demonstrate that the topographic theory is inadequate to explain the phenomena of dreaming and that it should be superseded for that purpose by the structural theory.

TOPOGRAPHIC THEORY OF DREAMS

Freud's exposition of the explanation for the phenomena of dreaming offered by the topographic theory is to be found

[115]

principally in Chapter VII of *The Interpretation of Dreams* (1900), in the chapters on dreams in the *Introductory Lectures on Psychoanalysis* (1916-1917), and in "A Metapsychological Supplement to the Theory of Dreams" (1917a). It may be summarized as follows.

Sleep is characterized by decathexis of the mental apparatus with consequent quiescence of its functions. This occurs in accordance with the wish to sleep of the systems *Cs.* and *Pcs.* However, since the part of the system *Ucs.* which we call the repressed is barred from access to the system *Pcs.*, it is likewise independent of the influence of the system *Pcs.* The energies of the repressed therefore remain active even during sleep, and its contents retain their cathexes. Also, some energies and contents of the system *Pcs.* are not entirely quiescent during sleep at times (e.g., "cares of the day," abandoned or unfinished trains of thought). Since mental energies in general press for discharge, the repressed of the system *Ucs.* and the active day residues of the system *Pcs.* strive for discharge during sleep, threatening thereby to disturb or waken the sleeper. During sleep, though, the muscular apparatuses under the control of the system *Cs.* are decathected and hence quiescent, so that energies active during sleep cannot pursue a normal course of discharge via the system *Pcs.* to the system *Cs.*, thereby achieving consciousness and motor expression or gratification or both. The active mental energies of the sleeper which correspond to the latent content of the dream about to be formed find the normal course of discharge closed to them and pursue instead a retrograde course. This course was normal in infancy, but is no longer so in waking life once the systems *Pcs.* and *Cs.* have developed and have assumed their rightful roles in the functioning of the mind. This retrograde course leads to the sensory end of the mental apparatus instead of to its motor end. Thus during sleep the mental energies which have remained active pass in a reverse direction through the system *Ucs.,* along associational pathways which lead from one to another memory trace. Their ready displacement in this fashion is characteristic of what happens to mental energies in the system *Ucs.* It will be recalled (see Chapter 2) that in that system the laws of the primary process hold sway: displacement and condensation. Thus the mental energies in question, which are about to give rise to a dream, move (are displaced) from one memory trace of the system *Ucs.* to another until all of the active energies have been concentrated on a few memory traces, usually visual ones. The resultant hypercathexis of these few traces causes them to become conscious as sensory images. It is these sensory images which constitute the manifest dream, which the dreamer takes to be real, since we are accustomed to believe in the reality of sensory impressions when they appear as such in consciousness.

We see, therefore, that the dream work is governed by the laws of the primary process, i.e., by displacement and condensation, as well as by a preference for visual memory traces, what Freud (1900) called the need to represent thoughts in visual (plastic) form. In addition, the dream work is influenced by two other agencies or tendencies of the mind. The first of these is the dream censor, which is the same as the intersystemic censor of waking life. This censor is still active during sleep, though its strength is diminished in sleep as compared with waking life. The second is the tendency to secondary revision, a term alternatively translated as secondary elaboration. Secondary revision designates the particular activity of the dreamer's mind which tends to organize the thoughts and images of the dream into a coherent and logical sequence. It should be noted, however, that the

[117]

sequences and other formal characteristics of the manifest dream do not always result from secondary revision. They may at times be determined primarily by the latent content of the dream. For example, a repetition of an image may signify emphasis, or the fact that a dream is in three parts may be due to the fact that the repressed wishes from which it stemmed were phallic ones.

The infantile nature of the dream work was clear to Freud from the start. This is apparent from the section on regression in Chapter VII of *The Interpretation of Dreams*. The essentials of this section have been summarized earlier in Chapter 6. What we wish to emphasize at this point will to some extent repeat what was said earlier in that chapter and in the chapter on the primary and secondary processes. It is that the topographic theory uses the concept of *systemic (topographic) regression* to account for the fact that the mental processes involved in the dream work are infantile as compared with the mental processes of normal, adult, waking life. This point is made particularly clearly in "A Metapsychological Supplement to the Theory of Dreams." According to the topographic theory, the infantile mode of mental functioning, the so-called primary process (i.e., the process which first holds sway in the mind), is confined to and characteristic of the system *Ucs.* The more mature mode of mental functioning, the secondary process, which gradually develops only later in life and which is normally dominant during waking life in the adult, is equally characteristic of the system *Pcs.* Thus the infantile character of the mental processes of the dream work is readily accounted for by postulating that the dream work takes place in the system *Ucs.*, i.e., in accordance with the infantile mode of mental functioning called the primary process. It is important for our later discussion to note that according to this explanation the infantile nature of mental functioning during the dream work is the result of a uniform and complete regression from the system *Pcs.* (secondary process) to the system *Ucs.* (primary process). By "uniform" we mean to indicate that all the aspects of mental functioning which are regressively altered in this way are equally altered. By "complete" we mean that the shift from the secondary process to the primary process is a total one, since the two processes are conceived by the topographic theory to be qualitatively distinct, rather than the extremes of a continuous spectrum.

STRUCTURAL THEORY OF DREAMS

Previous attempts to apply the structural theory to the phenomena of dreaming in a systematic way have been rare. The first such attempt seems to have been that of Brenner (1955a). The ideas contained in it will not be summarized here, since they will be incorporated in the discussion to follow. More recently Richardson and Moore (1963) have demonstrated the value of a systematic application of the structural theory to dream psychology in an interesting study of the dreams of psychotic patients.

We may begin our attempt to formulate a theory of dream psychology which is based on the concepts of the structural theory by recalling certain of the ways in which the structural theory differs from the topographic one in its concepts of mental functioning in general. We shall naturally be chiefly interested in those differences which will require some alteration in the theory of dream psychology which has just been outlined above on the basis of the topographic theory.

First, the principle of multiple functioning (Waelder, 1930) occupies an important place in the structural theory.

According to that principle, energies from the id, as they press for discharge, activate various ego and superego functions, functions which may erect countercathectic barriers to the discharge of the id energies in question, may expedite their discharge, or may direct or control them. The final result is thus multiply determined by id, ego, and superego tendencies, including among ego tendencies those functions which are concerned with the facts of external reality.

Second, it will be remembered that, unlike the topographic theory, the structural theory does not model the mental apparatus after a reflex arc. It does not postulate a normally progressive path of mental energies to follow which begins at the sensory end of the apparatus and terminates at its motor end. On the contrary, as just noted, psychic events in general are viewed as the result of a mutual interaction among forces or tendencies of the id, ego, and superego. The result of this interaction may be ideational, motor, or both; it may or may not reach consciousness, with or without an affective accompaniment. The point here at issue is that whatever the result, the path or direction of discharge is the same. It is not in one direction when a motor act results, and in the reverse direction when the result is a dream or waking hallucination.

Third, primitive or infantile modes of thinking and of mental functioning in general are not considered to be exclusively characteristic of one or another division of the mental apparatus. Infantile modes of thinking, often referred to as primary-process thinking or mentation, are characteristic not only of the id but of many processes of the ego and superego as well, both normally and pathologically (see Chapter 7). We know that primitive modes of ego functioning can contribute to highly valued activities, such as artistic or scientific creativity, for example, as well as to jokes, to play, and the like. In these cases, as we have noted earlier, we speak of regression of ego functioning in the service of the ego (Kris, 1934). Thus it will not be necessary for the structural theory to explain such phenomena as condensation and displacement in dreams by attributing the dream work exclusively to one division of the mental apparatus. It will instead emphasize the part played in the dream work by ego regression.

Bearing in mind the points just listed, how shall we proceed to formulate a theory of dream psychology on the basis of the structural theory?

First of all we may note that, like the topographic theory, the structural theory assumes that despite the general quiescence of function during sleep there are certain energies of the mind which remain active.[1]

Second, according to the structural theory, the mental energies which remain active during sleep initiate dreaming. They, and the mental processes associated with them, constitute the latent content of the ensuing dream. This latent content derives from the instinctual derivatives of the id on the one hand and from the impressions and cares of the preceding day on the other.

Thus far we see that the structural theory of dreams is essentially identical with that of the topographic theory. However, when we leave the question of the initiation of a dream and of its latent content, and turn instead to the dream work, this congruity no longer holds true.

The structural theory assumes that the energy associated with the latent dream content activates various unconscious

[1] The recent electroencephalographic studies of dreaming suggest that these energies are active during a particular stage of sleep only, rather than throughout its duration (for references see Fisher and Dement, 1963). However, this qualification is not decisive for our present purpose.

ego and superego functions just as might happen during waking life. Some of the ego functions assist or guide the instinctual energies toward satisfaction,[2] while other ego functions, e.g., the defenses, oppose the gratification just referred to, acting in conjunction with superego demands. However, it is also possible for superego demands to join forces with an id impulse, e.g., a masochistic or a sadistic one, as well as for the defensive functions of the ego to be directed against the prohibitions or demands of the superego, just as they may be against id derivatives. In other words, the dream work consists of an interplay, often a very complicated one, though at other times quite simple, among id, ego, and superego, of which the final result is the manifest dream.

It will be noted that this interplay, however simple or complicated it may be, is no different from what happens when an instinctual impulse is activated during waking life. During waking life as well as during sleep, what finally happens in the individual's mental life is the result of an interplay among the conflicting and cooperating tendencies of id, ego, and superego.[3] Yet the end result of this interplay in waking life is not a dream. How can one account for this difference in terms of the structural theory?

Our answer is as follows. (1) There is a regressive alteration

[2] Since the individual whose mental processes we are describing is asleep, instinctual satisfaction will ordinarily be essentially limited to a fantasy of instinctual gratification. This limitation does not always hold, however. The most striking example of this is that of a sexual orgasm during a dream, but there may also be coordinated muscular movements of various sorts, including chewing, sucking, or swallowing, or there may be tears, salivation, vocalization, urination or defecation, etc. In other words, instinctual discharge during sleep, though it characteristically gives rise to a wish-fulfilling fantasy, need not be limited to fantasy alone. It may also result in various gross somatic manifestations.

[3] This principle applies with equal force to parapraxes (Brenner, 1955b).

in many of the functions of the ego during dreaming. (2) There is a similar regressive alteration in superego functioning during dreaming. (3) Instinctual wishes and fantasies stemming from the id play a larger role in dreaming than they do in most adult, waking, mental phenomena. We shall discuss each of these points in turn.

With respect to regression of ego functions, we assume that this is a consequence of the sleeping state (Freud, 1917a). Perhaps, as noted above, it is a consequence of a particular stage of sleep, identifiable electroencephalographically. More than this we cannot say about the cause of the regression of ego functions which is such a striking characteristic of the mental activity during dreaming, i.e., during the dream work and the perception of the manifest dream. We can say much more, however, by way of description of the nature of these regressive alterations and of their consequences. Let us begin by specifying, as far as possible, just what regressive changes characterize ego functions during sleep.

If we attempt to list the functions involved, we must certainly include reality testing, thinking, language, defenses, integrative ability, sensory perception, and motor control. Some of these obviously overlap, others might be subdivided, but since any list would be subject to some qualification, let us take the one just given and consider each of the items in it.

We shall begin with reality testing. More specifically, we are concerned with that aspect of reality testing which has to do with the ability to distinguish between what is perceived of the outer world and what is the result of something going on in one's own mind: the ability to distinguish (outer) fact from (inner) fancy. The dreamer is unable to do this.[4]

4 With occasional exceptions to be discussed below.

His ability to test reality has regressed to a stage character-istic of infancy, to a time of life when, as an infant, he was unable to distinguish between the events of the outer world and those of the inner one. Traces of this stage normally persist well into childhood, as witness the child's tendency to treat his fantasies and games as real at least during play-time. It is not rare for a young child to have an imaginary companion for many months or even years, a companion who is as real and present to the child as any of the objectively real persons of his environment. It is the regressive alteration of the function of reality testing that accounts for the fact that the conscious result of the dream work, i.e., the images of the manifest dream, are as real to the dreamer as are waking fantasies to the small child.

Since thinking and the use of language are so intimately associated, we may conveniently consider them together. There are numerous manifestations of the regressive altera-tion of these functions during dreaming. For example, the dreamer tends to think as the child does, in concrete, sensory images, usually visual ones, rather than in words, as is char-acteristic for adult, waking thought. This regression to an infantile mode of thought accounts for the fact that most manifest dreams consist of visual images: a dream is some-thing that the dreamer sees in his sleep. It will be recalled that Freud (1900) originally accounted for this character-istic of dreams by postulating a need for plastic represent-ability as one of the attributes of the dream work. In addi-tion to thinking in visual images, the dreamer deals with words and language in a regressive way. There is a clearly evident tendency in the dream work to play with words, to equate words that sound alike, and to pun, as there is in childhood. There is likewise clearly evident a regression in other, closely related aspects of thinking. The dream work is full of representation by allusion, representation by the opposite, representation of the whole by the part, or vice versa (Freud, 1900). In a word, the dream work is characterized by that type of mentation, normally dominant in childhood, which is generally referred to in the psychoanalytic literature as primary-process thinking. In particular, the dream work is characterized by the use of symbols in the psychoanalytic sense of the word. Finally, as Freud pointed out (1900), a realistic attitude toward time, toward space, and toward death, as well as the usual adult requirements of logic and syntax are grossly defective or absent. All of these changes are attributable to a regressive alteration of various aspects of the ego functions of language and of thinking. In each case we can observe that the dreamer's mind is functioning in a primitive or infantile manner.

The ego's integrative function is also regressively altered during sleep. Freud (1900) noted the participation of this function in the dream work from the start of his researches, identifying it at that time as the tendency to secondary revision or elaboration. However, despite many exceptions, dreams are not as a rule harmonized and integrated with respect to their various component parts to nearly the same degree as we expect ordinary waking thoughts, or even daydreams, to be. The dreamer, like the child, is less concerned with unity and consistency than is the waking adult, even though, as Freud noted, the integrative function of the ego plays a part in dream formation.

One of the most striking of the changes in ego functioning during dreaming, and the one most significant in clinical work, is the diminution of the ego's defenses. Freud related this diminution to the paralysis of motility during sleep: since action is impossible, wishes are not so dangerous. It seems likely, however, that more is involved than a realistic appraisal by the dreamer of the defensive value of his own immobility during sleep. The dreamer's diminished defensive opposition to his instinctual wishes does in fact resemble the limited defensive capacities of the ego of a small child. If this resemblance is significant, the diminution of ego defenses during dreaming should be considered to be at least in part a regressive alteration of the defensive function of the ego.

Finally, as we know, the ego functions of sensory perception and motor control are also profoundly altered during sleep. In the case of these two functions, however, it is not so clear that the alterations to be observed are due to regression. They seem to be due rather to a diminution or suspension of the particular ego function in question. For example, the nearly complete suspension of purposeful motor activity which is a regular concomitant of sleep does not seem to differ qualitatively from voluntary suspension of motor function during waking life. As far as we can judge, it does not involve regression to patterns of motor activity or quiescence which are characteristic of infancy or of early childhood.[5] Sensory perception during sleep seems likewise to be diminished or suspended, rather than to regress to an

[5] It may be objected that the fact that in sleep a positive Babinski reflex may appear is suggestive of a regression in the functioning of the motor apparatus on which ego control of motor activity is so very dependent, and that since there is evidence of regression in the motor apparatus it is sensible to assume that there is regression in ego functioning as well. A satisfactory evaluation of the validity of this argument must await more precise information concerning some of the pertinent facts. For example, does the Babinski reflex appear during the same stage of sleep as that in which the dream work takes place? The reverse might be true, i.e., it may be that the Babinski appears only during very deep sleep, whereas the dream work may perhaps go on only during light sleep, as the electroencephalographers suggest. It may also be that a more detailed knowledge concerning other aspects of motor functioning during sleep, e.g., somnambulism, would be pertinent to the question whether the alterations in the ego function of motility which are attendant upon sleep are properly to be considered regressive or not.

earlier pattern or mode of functioning. Indeed, we are familiar with instances in which the diminution of sensory perception during sleep appears to be a selective inattention to certain stimuli, inattention of a sort with which we are quite familiar in adult, waking, mental functioning. Thus, for example, a sleeping parent will waken promptly to a baby's cry, while ignoring other, louder noises, just as a waking person perceives some sounds while ignoring others.

It will be remembered from what has been said in the chapters on regression and on the primary and secondary processes that the regressive changes in ego function which we have been discussing can be viewed as the result of a diminution or stripping away of those relatively late acquisitions of mental life which impose on our thinking the requirements of syntax, logic, and a generally realistic attitude toward life. The infantile modes of mental activity which are so conspicuous in the dream work are not absent in normal, adult, waking life. On the contrary, their presence and influence are obvious and are by no means to be viewed with disrespect as Kris (1934) and others have emphasized (Brenner, 1955a). Thus the regressions in ego functioning characteristic of dreaming may be ascribed to a selective suppression or abandonment of function, one which affects later acquisitions more profoundly than it does earlier ones. We see here the aptness of Freud's (1917a) somewhat humorous analogy between the psychic changes incident to sleep and the physical preparations for it: the removal of clothes, eyeglasses, and other prosthetic appliances, and the resumption of the costume, or lack of it, of babyhood.

Another aspect of the diminution and regression of ego functions during sleep is that the degree to which it occurs with respect to any particular function may vary considerably from dream to dream and even from one part of a dream to another. This fact should occasion no surprise in analysts, who are used to observing evidences of such alterations from day to day and from minute to minute in their analytic patients. In dreams, as we shall see, the dream work may regressively utilize nonverbal, visual thinking in one part of a dream, while verbal thoughts, characteristic of mature mental functioning, appear in another part. Indeed, visual elements and verbal thoughts may appear in a manifest dream simultaneously. Thus, in applying the structural theory to the problem of dreaming, it is important to remember that according to the structural theory, regression of ego functions is both selective and variable.

One may also conclude from such detailed observations of ego functioning as those noted here that the dream work, like waking mentation, is characterized by the simultaneous interplay of mature and primitive or infantile ego functioning; to use more familiar, though less correct terms: the simultaneous interplay of primary- and secondary-process thinking. It is only that in waking life the more mature forms of ego functioning tend to predominate, while in the dream work less mature forms of ego functioning predominate; at least they are more conspicuous and relatively more important than they normally are in waking life. It is apparent from all of these considerations why the mental phenomena of waking life to which dreams bear the closest relationship are those in which there is a substantial degree of regression of ego functions: neurotic or psychotic symptoms, parapraxes, and the various instances of regression in the service of the ego, such as daydreams, jokes, etc.

So much for ego regression during dreaming. Superego functions also show clear evidence of regressive alteration during dreaming, though superego regression has attracted less general attention than has regression of such ego functions as defenses and reality testing. It appears, nevertheless, that superego regressions contribute substantially to the infantile character of the mental processes involved in the dream work and in the manifest dream as well. For example, when unpleasure accompanies the direct or distorted fantasy of instinctual gratification in a manifest dream, it is far more often anxiety than guilt. What would produce guilt or remorse in waking life is more apt to produce fear of punishment during a dream, just as it normally does during early childhood when the superego is still in process of formation. Similarly the dreamer, like the child, seems to be more nearly exclusively guided by *lex talionis* than is the waking adult. He is also more prone to project his guilt impulses onto the person of others, while he identifies himself with the disapproving and punishing judge, and finally, he is more likely to instinctualize punitive suffering, i.e., to react masochistically. It is apparent that each of these characteristics of dream life represents a regression on the part of the dreamer to a more infantile stage of superego development and functioning. Isakower (1939) and others have asserted that spoken words in the manifest content of a dream are related to the participation of superego function in the dream work. Such a relation is indicative of a regression during dreaming to a stage of superego development when commands and prohibitions were contained in the spoken words of the dreamer's parents and had not yet been internalized. Finally, one may surmise that the fact that instinctual wishes often find a more direct and conscious expression in dreams than would be permitted them in waking life bespeaks a diminution of the superego's functioning to a more childish level as well as a diminution of the ego's defenses. We must remember in this connection that the link between superego functioning and the institution and maintenance of anti-instinctual defenses by the ego is a particularly close one. The defenses against the drives are normally maintained by the ego at the behest of the superego, once the superego has been firmly established as a system of the mind.

Now for the third point that we proposed to discuss, namely, the fact that instinctual wishes and fantasies stemming from the id play a larger role in dreaming than they do in most adult, waking, mental phenomena. That this is true seems self-evident. The explanation for it seems equally evident: during sleep the mental representations of external reality are largely decathected. The only things that matter to us are our own wishes and needs. This is one aspect of what Freud (1917a) emphasized as the increase in narcissism during sleep. Since the instinctual fantasies which comprise the id aspect of the latent content of a dream are so largely infantile in content, it is understandable that they too convey an infantile character to the dream which they stimulate.

We may now summarize the theory of the dream within the framework of the structural theory which we have just outlined. We begin by repeating that despite the general quiescence of mental functioning during sleep certain energies of the mind remain active. These, and the mental processes associated with them, constitute the latent content of the dream. This latent content derives from the instinctual derivatives of the id on the one hand and from the impressions and the cares of the preceding day on the other. The dream work consists of a mutual interplay among the various tendencies of id, ego, and superego, tendencies which may reinforce one another, may cooperate with one another, or may oppose one another. Such an interplay occurs as a regular state of affairs during waking life as well. However, during sleep various ego and superego functions are regressively altered. Moreover, a relatively large part is played in the dream work by infantile, wish-fulfilling fantasies, since a relatively smaller part is played by the claims of external reality, which are largely decathected during sleep. As a result, mental activity during dreaming is much more infantile in many ways than is mental activity during waking life. Condensation, displacement, representation by allusion, by opposites, by symbols, representation in concrete, visual images, disregard for time, space and death, in a word all the familiar characteristics of the dream work are due to ego and superego regression, plus the infantile nature of much of the latent content from which the dream work takes its origin. Finally, it is as a result of regressive alteration of the ego function of reality testing that the dreamer believes that what he dreams is not fantasy, but reality.

SUPERIORITY OF THE STRUCTURAL THEORY OF DREAMS OVER THE TOPOGRAPHIC THEORY OF DREAMS

In this section we propose to compare the explanations of dreaming by the topographic and the structural theories in order to support our thesis that the latter should replace the former. For this purpose we have chosen to examine four features of dreaming which are readily observable, and to contrast the inadequacy of the topographic theory to explain the available data in each case with the satisfactory nature of the explanation offered by the structural theory. Following this we shall discuss the advantages which accrue in everyday clinical work from understanding the dream within the framework of the structural theory.

The four features of dreaming we shall discuss are (1) the dreamer's conviction that the dream is real; (2) punishment dreams; (3) censorship and secondary revision during the dream work; and (4) evidences of variation in regression during dreaming. We shall see that in the first two cases

Freud himself decided in favor of the explanatory concepts of the structural theory.

1. The topographic theory explains the dreamer's belief in the reality of the manifest dream by the fact that the elements of the manifest dream are sensory images (Freud, 1900, 1917a). The dreamer, accustomed to accepting the testimony of his senses as proof of reality, believes the manifest dream is real: seeing is believing. However, Freud rejected this explanation as inadequate to explain the facts. He wrote, "we are quite familiar with situations in which a process of regressive reflection brings to consciousness very clear visual mnemic images, though we do not on that account for a single moment take them for real perceptions" (1917a, p. 231).[6] He went on to say that we could readily conceive the possibility that the dream work might do the same, so that its results would be a wishful fantasy that would be very appealing, but which would not be real to the dreamer. The explanation which he proposed in place of the one given by the topographic theory derives from the structural theory, even though in 1917 a published statement of the structural theory was still six years in the future. What determines whether visual images are accepted as real or not, Freud wrote, is the operation of the capacity for reality testing. Of this capacity he said, "We shall place reality-testing among the major *institutions of the ego,* alongside the censorships" (1917a, p. 233; italics in the original).

2. Freud discussed punishment dreams in addenda to *The Interpretation of Dreams* contained in the 1911, 1919, and 1930 editions of that work, as well as in "Remarks on the Theory and Practice of Dream-Interpretation" (1923b), which would have been incorporated into the main text in

[6] For an additional reference to such phenomena, see section iii of "Constructions in Analysis" (Freud, 1938).

1923 except for the expense involved in a new edition. In 1911 Freud related punishment dreams to masochistic tendencies.[7] Later, however, he expressly contradicted this earlier statement. In 1919 and 1923 he wrote that punishment dreams are not to be attributed to a repressed, instinctual wish, i.e., to masochism, but rather to the operation of the self-critical agency of the ego, and in the 1930 edition of *The Interpretation of Dreams* he referred to this agency by the term currently familiar to us, i.e., the superego. Here then is a second instance where Freud considered an explanation offered by the topographic theory to be inadequate and where he substituted for it an explanation by the structural theory.

3. Freud observed that both the censor and the need for secondary revision (in structural terms, both the integrative function of the ego and the ego's defenses) operate throughout the dream work. He wrote "We must assume . . . that from the very first the demands of this second factor [i.e., the factor of secondary revision] constitute one of the conditions which the dream must satisfy and that this condition, like those laid down by condensation, the censorship imposed by resistance, and representability, operate simultaneously in a conducive and selective sense upon the mass of material present in the dream-thoughts" (1900, p. 499). Yet the idea that the dream work takes place in the system *Ucs.*, which is so fundamental to the explanation of the dream offered by the topographic theory, makes it impossible to explain satisfactorily how the progress of the dream work can be so

---

[7] In addition, Freud pointed out that a pleasure-giving wish might be present in the latent content of a punishment dream. In the case of the examples he cited, which he called "parvenu" dreams, he detected in the latent content the wish to be young again, as though the dreamer was thinking, "It's true I was poor and lowly then, but I was young; my whole life was before me!"

influenced. Both the demand for secondary revision and the censor are mental functions which the topographic theory attributes to the system *Pcs*. The demand for secondary revision requires that mental processes in the systems *Pcs*. and *Cs*. must conform to certain requirements of logic, causality, etc., while the censor bars from access to the system *Pcs*., and through it to the system *Cs*., whatever mental processes belonging to the system *Ucs*. are in conflict with the demands of the censor. How, therefore, is either factor to be conceived of as influencing the dream work, the flux of energies *within* the system *Ucs*. itself, i.e., of functioning within that system, and of doing so long before there is any question of the energies of the system *Ucs*. intruding into the other systems of the mind?

It may properly be objected that the question just raised is a poorly phrased one. It supposes that the systems *Ucs*. and *Pcs*. are two distinct regions or provinces of the mind which may be analogized to distinct geographical areas. As Freud (1915b) pointed out, this supposition is really an oversimplification, though one that is convenient, and good enough for many purposes. The more correct statement of the topographic theory is that those mental phenomena which follow the laws of the primary process (condensation, displacement, tendency to immediate discharge) comprise the system *Ucs*.; those phenomena which as the result of a specific hypercathexis follow the laws of the secondary process (delay of discharge, conformity to external reality, logic, etc.), comprise the system *Pcs*. (see Chapter 2). But this correction or refinement makes it no easier to explain how the censor and the demand for secondary revision can influence the course of the dream work. If the dream work proceeds in the system *Ucs*., i.e., according to the primary process, how can it at the same time be proceeding according to the secondary process, under the influence of the censor and of the need for secondary revision of the system *Pcs.?* Whichever way we phrase our question we are confronted with a logical impasse. Freud was very clear about the facts: censorship and secondary revision do not operate only after the dream work within the system *Ucs.* is over. In most dreams, perhaps in all, they influence the course of the dream work within that system as well. Yet according to the topographic theory, the dream work takes place in the system *Ucs.,* i.e., according to the primary process, while the censoring tendencies and the need for secondary revision belong to the system *Pcs.* and therefore function according to the secondary process. It appears that the topographic theory does not fit the facts.

In the case of the structural theory, however, there is no such discrepancy between fact and theory. As we have several times noted, the structural theory explains the dream work as an interplay among id, ego, and superego. Thus it postulates that ego functions, in this case defenses and integrative functions, participate in the dream work throughout its course. We must remember that the structural theory was devised in order to offer a better explanation than could the topographic theory of the interaction among drive derivatives, anti-instinctual tendencies, and self-punitive tendencies within the mind. It is to be expected, therefore, that it accounts better than can the topographic theory for the aspects of the dream work which are under discussion here, just as it does for punishment dreams.

4. As has already been noted, it was clear to Freud as soon as he had first successfully penetrated the mysteries of dream interpretation that during dreaming the mind functions in a more primitive and infantile way than during waking life, i.e., that during the dream there occurs a profound regression in mental functioning. We have also noted that the

topographic theory accounts for this regression by locating the dream work in the system *Ucs.*, and that this means that according to the topographic theory the mental regression during dreaming is both uniform and complete. In fact, however, it is easy to observe when one examines the data that regression during dreaming is usually selective and often fluctuant. That is, not all ego and superego functions are usually equally involved, and the degree of regression of any single function may vary from moment to moment during dreaming.

As an example of fluctuation in the degree of regression of an ego function we may call attention to the fact that exceptionally, but by no means rarely, one or several elements of a manifest dream are not accepted as real by the dreamer. Instead they are accompanied by some such thought as, "This is only a dream." The topographic theory has a difficult time explaining this phenomenon. If the thought, "This is only a dream," is accepted as a part of the dream, then it cannot, in the framework of the topographic theory, be considered as a valid or meaningful comment by the dreamer any more than any other element of the manifest dream can be taken at face value. It must be considered to be the result of a process of condensation and displacement which has taken place in the system *Ucs.* and to be understandable only after the dreamer's associations have been obtained. Yet it was clear to Freud (1900, pp. 488-489) that the thought, "This is only a dream," could be a valid comment despite its appearance during the manifest dream. Indeed he correctly understood it to be motivated by the impending development of anxiety, or similar unpleasure, and to serve the function of avoiding such a development. As long as he had only the topographic theory to work with, however, Freud was forced to resolve the difficulty by making an arbitrary assumption. He removed the thought, "This is only a dream," from the realm of dream psychology and attributed it to the activity of a waking part of the mind, even though the thought had occurred during sleep. He wrote, "In my view the contemptuous critical judgement, 'it's only a dream', appears in a dream when the censorship, which is never quite asleep, feels that it has been taken unawares by a dream which has already been allowed through. It is too late to suppress it, and accordingly the censorship uses these words to meet the anxiety or the distressing feeling aroused by it. The phrase is an example of *esprit d'escalier*[8] on the part of the psychical censorship." The structural theory, on the other hand, has a simple and satisfactory explanation for this phenomenon without any need for recourse to an *ad hoc* explanation. The thought, "This is only a dream," indicates a change in the dreamer's ability to test reality. The degree of regression and consequent impairment, by adult standards, of this particular ego function has diminished for the time being, and the dreamer realizes that what he sees and thinks is not real, but a dream. Here is a case of fluctuation in degree of regression. It contradicts the topographic theory, but is readily explained by the structural one. We may add that the structural theory is wholly in harmony with Freud's keen observation concerning the motivation and function of the phenomenon in question. As Freud realized long ago, in most cases the temporary improvement in reality testing just described serves a defensive function: it prevents or minimizes the development of anxiety or of other unpleasure during a dream.

What we have just discussed is an example of fluctuation

---

8 Freud used the French phrase in the original, though there is an exactly equivalent German one: *Treppenwitz*. Heath defines it as "afterthought; cleverness after the event."

of the degree of regression of an ego function during dreaming. As an example of partial regression we may take the function of visual representation. We have noted that in most dreams thoughts are typically translated into concrete sensory terms, usually visual ones. This is evidenced by the fact that a manifest dream is typically something seen by the dreamer: it is a collection of visual images. But many dreams have not only sensory elements in the manifest content. Many have verbal thoughts as well which are of the ordinary, waking sort. For an example we have only to turn to the first dream in *The Interpretation of Dreams,* the familiar dream of Irma's injection. Here we find, half a dozen lines down in the text of the dream, the words, "I thought to myself that after all I must be missing some organic trouble." It is clear that this thought is not just a description of a visual image. It is part of the manifest content of the dream. In fact it is the content of a fear. A few pages farther on (p. 109), when Freud is giving his associations to each element of the dream, he restates this element in these words: "I was alarmed at the idea that I had missed an organic illness." Moreover, this element of the manifest dream is a result of the dream work, just as the visual elements are, and it is to be understood only from the dreamer's associations to it. In this case the associations given have to do with the wish to be free of any responsibility for Irma's incomplete cure, a wish which is fundamental to the whole of the dream. The latent content of the particular element that we have mentioned is given by Freud in these words: "If Irma's pains had an organic basis, once again I could not be held responsible for curing them;[9] my treatment only set out to get rid of *hysterical* pains" (p. 109).

[9] The translation in the *Standard Edition* is misleading. A more correct translation would read: "If Irma's pains had an organic basis, it would not be my obligation to cure them. . . ."

Such examples are not rare. Verbalized thoughts are often found in the manifest content of a dream along with its visual and other sensory elements. When we do find them we know from experience that they are not ordinarily to be taken at face value. Like dream images, verbalized thoughts which are a part of the manifest dream must be associated to if their meaning is to be discovered.[10] We see, therefore, that there are exceptions to the statement that in dreaming the ego functions of thought and language regress to the stage in which thoughts and ideas are expressed in visual images. Some of the latent dream content is in fact represented visually, far more of it than would be the case in waking life. But in many dreams, some at least of the latent content is represented by verbalized thoughts as it would be in waking life. In other words, here again is a regression which is not total and uniform, as the topographic theory would require, but is rather selective, as the structural theory predicts. The topographic theory of dreaming cannot account for the appearance of verbalized thoughts as such in a manifest dream. It must either ignore them or attribute them to some sort of mental functioning during sleep other than the dream work proper (Freud, 1900, pp. 488-489).

Illustrations of this point could be multiplied at will. In essence, what they do is to illustrate from examples in dream psychology what has already been said in Chapter 6 with respect to mental functioning in general, namely, that regression is characteristically selective and often fluctuant, rather than global and uniform.

It appears, therefore, that the structural theory has definite advantages over the topographic one as a basis for a theory of dream psychology. First, the structural theory explains better the dreamer's conviction that his dream is real while

10 The thought, "This is only a dream," is an exception to this rule.

he is dreaming it. Second, it affords a satisfactory explanation of punishment dreams. Third, it accounts for the participation of the censorship and of the need for secondary revision throughout the course of the dream work. Fourth, it accounts for the observation that the regression in mental functioning during dreaming is not complete and uniform, but is rather selective and variable. We may recall that Freud himself took note of the first two of these instances of the inadequacy of the topographic theory in explaining dreaming.

Now we ask what can be said of the practical value of viewing dreams within the framework of the structural theory rather than of the topographic one. Granted that it may be advantageous to do this as far as theory is concerned, what advantages accrue from doing so as far as day-to-day analytic work is concerned?

We may perhaps best answer this question by reviewing a bit of psychoanalytic history. In the early days of analysis the analyst's chief aim was to arrive at an understanding of his patient's unconscious, sexual wishes as quickly as possible. Any obstacles or resistances in the way of this goal were to be circumvented or overcome without ado, and dreams were highly prized for the assistance they offered the skilled analyst in discovering his patient's unconscious wishes. The idea that analyzing resistances in a systematic, genetically oriented way is an essential part of normal analytic procedure had yet to be clearly formulated. The aim was to get to the unconscious as quickly as possible, and the dream was the royal road to the unconscious.

The stages of development in the technique and goals of analysis that have supervened since those early days have already been discussed in Chapters 5 and 8. We shall not review them here. Their result has been that ego and super-ego analysis have come to be essential parts of our daily work alongside of their predecessor, which is today often called id analysis. We try today to understand the patient's inner *conflicts*, not merely the infantile *wishes* which comprise the instinctual aspect of those conflicts. We try to make clear to each patient both the anti-instinctual and the instinctual aspects of his conflicts and to trace the history of both back to the experiences and events of childhood which were decisively important in determining the original nature of his conflicts, their subsequent course, and their influence on the various aspects of his mental development.

We still welcome the aid dreams have to offer in id analysis. It may happen, for example, that the analysis of a dream will give the first clear indication of the nature of the instinctual wishes which a patient is unconsciously warding off by means of defenses which we are still in process of analyzing. But we have found that dream analysis can tell us much more about unconscious mental conflicts than merely the instinctual wishes involved in them. For example, when a patient dreams about a symptom, we expect to learn more about both sides of the conflict which underlies that symptom, and not only about the instinctual derivatives associated with it. Thus we expect to learn from the analysis of our patients' dreams about the nature of the fears associated with their instinctual wishes, about their unconscious need to punish themselves, and even about the defenses which at the moment they are unconsciously employing in their struggles against their wishes (see, for example, Arlow, 1953).

It seems fair to say that many, probably most analysts use dreams in these ways during their analytic work with patients. In so far as they do so, they are *in fact,* whether they realize it or not, applying the conceptual framework of the structural theory to the problems of dream psychology and dream interpretation. They are using dreams in the analysis of ego functions, e.g., defenses, as well as in the analysis of the superego, and no longer solely for id analysis. The fact that such usage is already so widespread should be the best answer to the question. "Is the structural theory superior to the topographic one with respect to the practical, everyday problems of dream analysis in psychoanalytic practice?"

We hope that we have accomplished our purpose: to show that the changes which distinguish the structural theory from the topographic one are essential to a satisfactory explanation of dreaming, and that the conceptual framework afforded by the structural theory is the more useful practically as well as theoretically. In pursuing this purpose we have had occasion to outline a theory of dream psychology using the conceptual framework of the structural theory as a base. Such an outline is long since overdue, and will, we hope, prove fruitful.

We may conclude this chapter by reminding the reader that Freud (1900) emphasized that the explanatory concepts which he proposed in Chapter VII of *The Interpretation of Dreams* were not derived from the study of dreams alone. On the contrary, they form a psychological theory, the topographic theory, as we call it now, which was derived from his study of neuroses[11] as well as of dreams, and which is as applicable to the mental processes involved in the genesis of neurotic symptoms as it is to the dream work (See Chapter 2).

Freud clearly stated his opinion that no theory of mental functioning could rest upon the study of a single category of mental phenomena, such as dreams, however profound the study in question might be. Dreams, according to Freud, must be related to other mental phenomena, phenomena

---

[11] Also, though less importantly, of jokes and of the psychopathology of everyday life.

which have been studied earlier and are better known, i.e., neurotic symptoms. By the same token, again according to Freud, one of the tasks of a theory of the mind, if it is to be considered a satisfactory theory, is to make clear to us the place which dreams and dreaming occupy in mental life with respect to other mental phenomena. Our theory should tell us what dreams have in common with such phenomena, as well as the ways in which they differ from them.

In attempting, therefore, to include dreams among those mental phenomena to which we apply the structural theory, we are in fact following the same course of action which Freud pursued more than half a century earlier. We are maintaining that a proper understanding of dreams requires that the theories we use explain or apply not only to dreams but to the wide range of other mental phenomena with which we are familiar as well, both normal and pathological; phenomena for the understanding, study, and treatment of which the structural theory is our best existing tool.

10

The Psychopathology
of the Psychoses

IN THIS CHAPTER we propose to review psychoanalytic theories concerning the psychopathology of the psychoses. Current psychoanalytic theories in this area, as in the case of dreams, date back to a period before the evolution of the structural theory. They have never been made consonant with the structural theory in a thorough or systematic fashion. We hope to demonstrate the necessity as well as the value of revising our theories of the psychopathology of the psychoses to ensure their consonance with the structural theory and with its corollaries, the dual instinct theory and the theory of anxiety as a signal of danger.

The lack of consonance just referred to may not be apparent. Even a brief survey of the literature reveals scores of books and articles published during the past four decades which have applied to the understanding of the psychoses the theory of aggression, ego psychology, and the current theory of anxiety and defense. Freud himself wrote two brief papers, "Neurosis and Psychosis" (1924a) and "The Loss of Reality in Neurosis and Psychosis" (1924b), which are the first attempts to apply the structural theory to the psychopathology of the psychoses. These have been followed by many contributions by other analysts, not a few of which have made major additions to our understanding of the problems with which we are concerned in this chapter. Nevertheless, we believe it is correct to say that much remains to be done in bringing our current theories of psychoses into line with Freud's major theoretical contributions of the 1920s.

We may best begin our attempt to document this assertion by reviewing briefly Freud's own formulations concerning the psychopathology of the psychoses. In order to understand Freud's ideas on this subject, it is necessary to realize, first of all, that they rest on the assumption (Freud, 1924c) that the psychic processes in psychoses and in neuroses display a fundamental unity. Psychoses are not a thing apart. What psychoanalysis had already discovered about the neuroses, Freud proposed to apply to the study of the psychoses. This fundamental premise implies what was revolutionary half a century ago, though it is commonplace now, namely, that the symptoms of psychotic patients make sense in the same way as do the symptoms of neurotic patients and the dreams of normal persons. That is to say, if one knows the context of the individual's life in which the symptoms have appeared and particularly if one can elicit the individual's associations to the symptoms, then one can discover what were the intelligible, though often unconscious, wishes, fears, and fantasies that gave rise to them. More than that, in thus understanding, or interpreting, the symptoms one can hope to gain insight into the forces within the mind which were responsible for the transformation of coherent, intelligible ideas into psychotic symptoms. One can gain the clues that are essential for an understanding of those mental processes which constitute the psychopathology of the psychoses.

These were the assumptions which determined Freud's

basic attitude toward the problems which the psychoses presented to him. It was with them in mind that he approached the myriad symptoms which psychotic patients present to any investigator who attempts to understand the psychoses from their clinical aspects. But which of the patients' many symptoms were the ones on which Freud focused? Which seemed to him to be the *essential* characteristics of the psychoses, the characteristics which differentiate them from their close relatives, the neuroses? It is clear that whatever constitutes the essence of psychosis is of central importance in its pathology. Consequently, the selection of what is essential from among the multitude of observable phenomena is of very great importance in formulating a theory. It may be recalled, for example, that Kahlbaum emphasized motor phenomena in schizophrenics; Kraepelin, the progressive course ending in dementia; and Bleuler, the thought disorder and affective disturbance. What did Freud choose to emphasize?

The feature of psychosis which Freud decided is of principal importance is the change in the patient's relationship with the persons and other objects of the world about him. He was impressed by the clinically verifiable observation that, generally speaking, there is a withdrawal from the environment which is reflected in both behavioral and subjective changes. Psychotic patients characteristically are less interested in the persons in their environment than they were before their illnesses began. Often they are extremely remote and detached from the whole of the world about them as far as their behavior is concerned: silent, solitary, and unresponsive, even to those whom they formerly loved. In some cases their whole relationship with their environment becomes primarily a negative or hostile one, characterized by suspicion, fear, and violence. When it is possible to learn what such withdrawn psychotic patients are thinking, one often discovers that they have the idea that the world about them and the people in it have somehow changed. At times they believe the world has been destroyed, at times that everything and everybody is unreal, etc. It is this group of familiar symptoms, to which he referred as the patient's break with reality, that Freud (1924b; 1932a, p. 27; 1940, pp. 97-99) considered to constitute the most characteristic single feature of the psychoses. How did he propose to explain it? What did he consider its psychopathology to be?

In accordance with the tendency that was uppermost in his theoretical orientation at the time, Freud (1911b) proposed an explanation in which the major emphasis fell on a quantitative or economic factor: the distribution of the patient's libidinal cathexes. The break with reality, he suggested, can be explained as a consequence of the patient having withdrawn his libidinal cathexes from the mental representations (memories, fantasies, wishes, etc.) of the objects, i.e., of the persons and things, in the world about him. To a psychotic patient who has thus decathected object representations, Freud reasoned, the real objects which correspond to those representations have lost all interest. They no longer exist for him. They are unreal or destroyed. Thus the break with reality is to be explained as the result of a shift of the patient's available libido away from object representations, or, in other words, away from the mental representations of the external world. It was in this way that Freud (1911b) explained what he considered to be the most characteristic single feature of the psychoses.

At the same time, the idea of a quantitative shift of libido away from object representations enabled Freud (1911b) to offer a simple and plausible explanation for two other important clinical features of the psychoses: megalomania and hypochondriasis. He reasoned as follows. What happens to

[147]

the libido that has been detached from object representations? Perhaps it is bound by being attached to the patient's own self. If one assumes this to be the case, then one can explain in the following way the fact that psychotic patients are so self-centered, often to the degree of megalomania, and that they are so frequently hypochondriacal. Just as decathexis leads to loss of interest, so hypercathexis leads to excessive interest. The patient's hypercathexis of his self or ego (in German the two words are the same) leads to megalomania. Hypercathexis of a body organ, on the other hand, leads to hypochondriasis. Hypochondriasis was thus considered by Freud to be similar in mechanism to the actual neuroses, specifically to anxiety neurosis. In both conditions he postulated an excessive accumulation of libido, and in both he assumed that this libido was transformed into anxiety. Thus it appeared to Freud that a considerable number of the symptoms of psychosis could be explained as due essentially to shifts in quantities of libido away from their investment (cathexis) in object representations to a cathexis of the patient's self.

At the same time we may assume that it was apparent to Freud that regression also plays an important part in the psychopathology of the psychoses. He had long been impressed by the significance of the similarities between dreams and psychoses (Freud, 1900, 1908). The mental processes of psychotic patients obviously show all of the infantile traits which the topographic theory attributes to the functioning of the system *Ucs*.

It was at this point that Freud introduced the concept of narcissism.[1] He assumed that there is a very early phase in the

[1] In his introductory note to Freud's essay "On Narcissism," Strachey observed that Freud's first published reference to narcissism was in 1910 in connection with the psychology of male homosexuality. Either simultaneously, or soon thereafter, it became an important part of his theory of the psychopathology of the psychoses.

libidinal development of every individual which is characterized by the fact that it is the individual's own self which is primarily, perhaps exclusively, cathected with libido. Object representations, in so far as they exist at all, are either not yet differentiated by the infant from himself, or are very little cathected in comparison with himself. At this stage in his life the individual is normally self-centered, has little interest in objects except as they directly concern himself, is much concerned with his own bodily sensations and functions, and exhibits various of the traits of thinking which are so characteristic of the psychotic patient and of the dreamer. In other words, Freud correctly perceived the profound similarities between the psychotic patient and the infant and proposed to explain the similarity in terms of libido theory. He assumed that in both the psychotic patient and the infant cathexes of object representations are either nonexistent or are insignificant compared with the amount of libido which cathects the individual himself.

We see, therefore, that in Freud's theory regression and the economy of libido were closely related. The psychotic patient's break with reality, his megalomania, and his hypochondriasis are all explained as due to the fact that object representations have been decathected and that the libido which previously cathected object representations now cathects the patient's self. This change in the distribution or economy of the patient's libido may be described as a shift from a normal libidinal position to a narcissistic one. It constitutes a regression to the stage of narcissism through which every normal child was assumed to pass very early in his life.

It should be added that the narcissistic regression just referred to was considered to explain more than the psychotic patient's break with reality, megalomania, and hypochondriasis. It was believed to explain many of the other infantile characteristics of his mental functioning as well, since it was assumed that a libidinal regression entails regression of what today we call ego functions as well (see Chapter 6). To be sure, even in 1911 Freud noted that libidinal shifts probably could not explain all the important phenomena of the psychology of the psychoses. Even at that early date he postulated that ego factors, as yet obscure, probably play an important part. In other words, we must bear in mind that the concept of narcissism is more than an amplification of the theory of the instinctual drives. It is equally valid to consider narcissism as one of the essential, early steps in the gradual development by Freud of his concept of the ego and of the structural theory as a whole. Nevertheless, the fact remains that at the time he first introduced the term narcissism, Freud's theory of the psychopathology of the psychoses was based largely on assumptions concerning the economy of the libido.

The role played in this theory by the concept of narcissistic regression goes still further than we have yet indicated, however. Freud assumed that the psychotic patient, at least in many cases, does not remain permanently and totally in a narcissistic state. In this respect one might say that the course of his illness resembles the normal course of development of the infant who is in the narcissistic phase of life. The infant normally develops what we call object relations. This process is explained by the assumption that narcissistic libido is transformed into object libido. It is directed toward the mental representations of external objects, i.e., it cathects object representations. Freud (1911b) observed that, after an initial period of withdrawal, psychotic patients may also re-establish contact of a sort with the outer world, albeit a pathological one, characterized by delusions and hallucinations. He explained the observed sequence of clinical events by assuming that the psychotic patient tends to transform at least some of his narcissistic libido into object libido just as does the infant in the stage of narcissism.

This constitutes what Freud called the restitutive phase of the psychosis. The patient's libido, which was withdrawn from object representations in the regressive stage of his illness, is restored to them in the second stage, i.e., the restitutive phase.[2] It is important to recognize that Freud used the word "restitution" to mean the restoration of libidinal cathexes of the mental representations of objects, cathexes which had been previously withdrawn. He did not use "restitution" to refer to behavior toward an actual object itself or to a fantasy about such an object. It did not refer, for example, to penitent behavior, or to a fantasy or a delusion of saving someone or of bringing him back to life.

We may repeat Freud's (1911b, 1914a) theory of the psychopathology of the psychoses in a somewhat more systematic form as follows. There is a fundamental unity, according to Freud, between the mental processes in psychoses and neuroses. Despite their fundamental similarity in other respects, however, he noted that they differ from one another in certain important ways. These differences he conceptualized in terms of regression and of libidinal economy. He postulated that psychotic patients are unconsciously fixated to an earlier phase of libidinal development than are neurotic ones, namely, to the narcissistic phase. When they regress, therefore, they regress to the narcissistic phase, i.e., more deeply than do neurotic patients.

In terms of libidinal economy, Freud assumed that psy-

2 Freud emphasized that the recathexis of object representations during the restitutive phase is incomplete and abnormal. He assumed that in this phase only the object representations of the system *Pcs.* are recathected. Those of the system *Ucs.*, he assumed, remain uncathected.

choses are characterized by a two-stage process. In the first stage, which corresponds to the narcissistic regression just mentioned, the mental representations of external objects are decathected. The libido thus freed is assumed to cathect the patient's self. In the second, or restitutive stage, there is an attempt to recathect object representations. This attempt is assumed to be successful only in those patients who recover from their illness. In other patients it is assumed to be incomplete or abortive.

Freud considered the decathexis of object representations which characterizes the first stage of a psychosis to be the analogue of neurotic repression. Thus he considered one essential difference between the neuroses and the psychoses to be that the process of repression in the two conditions is not the same. In the adult neurotic, repression is a mental mechanism which results in barring from consciousness the event which precipitated the patient's neurosis as well as the instinctual wishes and fantasies which are associated with it. The psychotic patient reacts similarly, according to Freud, but in his case repression is a more profound and far-reaching process. It does not result simply in barring certain ideas and memories, certain mental representations as we say, from access to consciousness. It results in a profound change in the mental representations themselves. In other words, neurotic repression does not deprive repressed mental representations (memories, wishes, and other ideas) of their libidinal excitation. On the contrary, in neurotic patients repressed mental representations remain strongly cathected with libido. In fact, they bring about a failure of repression by forcing their way into consciousness in the distorted form which we recognize as a neurotic symptom. Freud assumed that the process of repression in psychotic patients, on the other hand, actually decathects the repressed mental representations. The libidinal excitation which was formerly attached to them has been withdrawn; they are without libidinal charge and, as a consequence, the objects of the environment to which they correspond are deprived of their former importance and meaning to the individual. They have lost all emotional significance. They no longer exist for him.

It was in this way that Freud explained the clinically observable fact of the psychotic patient's break with reality. By making the further assumption that the libido which has been detached from the mental representations of objects is directed toward the patient's self, he explained the symptoms of grandiosity and hypochondriasis. If the detached libido cathects a body organ, hypochondriasis results. If it cathects the self (the ego), megalomanic symptoms follow. Delusions and hallucinations, on the other hand, Freud explained as being due to attempts to recathect object representations which characterize the second, or restitutive, phase of the psychotic patient's illness.

The description of the psychopathology of the psychoses which we have just outlined is still accepted by the great majority of psychoanalysts. It is true, as noted above, that in recent years most, if not all, analysts have applied to the problem of the psychopathology of schizophrenia Freud's more recent theories of mental functioning as well, i.e., ego psychology, the theory of aggression, and the theory of anxiety and of the defenses. As we have already observed, a great deal has been said and written during the past forty years about disturbances of ego functions in schizophrenia, about ego weakness, about anxiety and defense in relation to schizophrenic symptoms, about superego abnormalities, about instinct defusion and aggression, and about various aspects of object relations, especially orality, within the framework of the structural theory. However, all of these contributions appear to have been in the nature of additions to the theory just summarized, or of elaborations of various aspects of it. Each of the contributors appears to have held fast to the two ideas, both basically important to Freud's early formulation: (1) that in schizophrenia the psychosis is initiated by the withdrawal of libidinal cathexes from objects, a form of defense (repression, as Freud originally called it) which is per se pathological; and (2) that this first stage of the illness is generally followed by a second, restitutive phase which is characterized by the appearance of delusions and hallucinations. All agree with Freud that the essence of schizophrenia is a break with reality, and that the explanation for this break is a decathexis of the mental representations of some or all of the objects of the outer world. To cite but a single example, in Fenichel's (1945) *Psychoanalytic Theory of Neurosis,* the chapter on schizophrenia is divided into two sections of which the first is titled the regressive phase and the second the restitutive phase.[3]

It is our thesis that neither of the two assumptions just mentioned is warranted today, and that neither should be retained as an integral part of the psychoanalytic theory of the psychoses. We hope to show (1) that they are contradicted by clinical observation; and (2) that the later concepts of Freud's structural theory, particularly the concept of regression of ego functions, explain the clinical phenomena of the psychoses better than do his earlier concepts of libidinal decathexis and recathexis. We believe that a reformulation of the psychopathology of the psychoses which is more con-

---

[3] The description of M. Klein and her followers of the mental processes of the neonate are considered by them to be directly related to the psychopathology of the psychoses, as their terminology indicates: paranoid position; depressive position. An adequate discussion of M. Klein's theories as they apply to the psychology of the psychoses is beyond the scope of the present chapter.

sistent with the conceptual framework of the structural theory offers both theoretical and therapeutic advantages.

Let us proceed to such a reformulation. It may be outlined as follows. We start from the proposition which Freud emphasized: namely, that there is a basic unity between the psychopathology of the psychoses and that of the neuroses. Important parts are played in both by infantile trauma and fixation, as well as by later conflict with consequent regression and other defensive reactions. What particularly characterizes the mental processes in psychosis, however, and what tends, therefore, to distinguish the psychopathology of the psychoses from that of the neuroses appear to be the following.

1. In psychoses the degree of instinctual regression or of instinctual infantilism, as the case may be, tends to be greater than in the neuroses. Psychotic patients more often than neurotic ones, and usually to a greater degree, show evidence of regression to prephallic (pregenital) instinctual aims. They are also more likely to show evidence of the persistence to an unusual degree of prephallic wishes and gratification throughout childhood and into adult life. It should be emphasized, however, that the differences between psychotic patients and neurotic ones with respect to their instinctual lives are differences of degree. Many, probably most, psychotic patients have severe conflicts of a phallic nature, as well as the prephallic ones just referred to. Current psychoanalytic literature on the psychoses, with its emphasis on oral and anal instinctual wishes and conflicts, gives the impression of underestimating the importance of phallic drive derivatives in the psychopathology of psychotic patients.

2. The instinctual life of the psychotic, in addition to being more infantile than that of the neurotic, is more aggressive as well. It will be recalled that Freud (1923a) postulated a connection between these two phenomena. He suggested

that instinctual regression regularly leads to instinctual defusion. When defusion occurs, aggressive instinctual derivatives presumably play a more important part in mental life. In any case, it is clear, as many authors have noted, that manifestations of aggression and of conflicts over aggression are of very great importance in the psychopathology of the psychoses.

3. Psychotic patients generally show evidence of more severe and more widespread disturbance of ego and superego functions than do neurotic ones. Such disturbances may be either regressive or of the nature of maldevelopments. It appears that maldevelopments of ego and superego functions predominate in cases of psychosis in infancy and childhood. Since such clinical conditions are still less thoroughly studied than are psychoses in adults, and since our own clinical experience has been nearly exclusively with adult psychotic patients, we shall consider only the latter in the discussion which follows. Though maldevelopment, or infantilism, of ego and superego functions may play a significant role in certain cases of psychosis in adult life, it seems that a far larger role, at least in most cases, is to be attributed to regressive alterations of ego and superego functions.[4] We wish to emphasize that what is of particular importance is that these regressive alterations generally serve as defenses against the emergence or the development of anxiety in situations of intrapsychic conflict.

It may be noted in passing that Freud (1924b) recognized that disturbances of ego functions occur regularly both in the neuroses and in the psychoses. He likewise appreciated that these disturbances are more extensive in themselves and

---

[4] Hartmann (1950b, 1953) has called attention to the importance of studying the genetic factors which are presumably responsible for the predisposition to regression of ego functions in adult life.

have more serious consequences for the individual who is psychotic than is likely to be the case in the neurotic patient. However, it was not possible in 1924 to recognize clearly that the disturbances in ego functions that occur in the psychoses (and, for that matter, in the neuroses as well) are primarily defensive in nature, nor to understand their precise relationship to anxiety. Instead, they were explained either as indirect consequences of repression (decathexis of object representations), or as results of regression to the narcissistic phase of instinctual life. It was not until 1926 that Freud was able to recognize the role of anxiety in mental conflict, as well as to understand more clearly the defensive functions of the ego (Freud, 1926, 1932a; A. Freud, 1936). These concepts form the basis of present-day psychoanalytic theories of the psychopathology of the neuroses as well as of normal and pathological character development. We believe that they are equally important and valuable in understanding the psychopathology of the psychoses.

To repeat, the great majority of the alterations in the ego and superego functions which characterize the psychoses are part of the individual's defensive efforts in situations of inner conflict and are motivated by a need to avoid the emergence of anxiety, just as is the case in normal and in neurotic conflicts. In the psychoses the defensive alterations in ego functions are often so extensive as to disrupt the patient's relationship with the world about him to a serious degree. Such a disruption is the break with reality to which Freud (1911b) so early called attention and which he explained by assuming that object representations had been decathected.

Moreover, it seems more accurate to speak of defensive disturbances in various ego functions in psychosis rather than to consider a break with reality or a loss of object relations to be a universal and distinguishing feature of the onset of such conditions. The reason for this is as follows. It is true that most psychotic patients do show severe disturbances early in their illness in their relation to the people and other objects in the world about them, but there is a significant minority in whom this is not the case. What seems to be common to all psychotic patients is that various ego functions are disturbed as part of the defensive struggle against instinctual derivatives, self-punitive trends, or both. If many ego functions are severely disturbed, the individual's capacity to adapt to his environment in a socially acceptable way is almost sure to be compromised. Nevertheless, it is important to the understanding and to the treatment of any individual case to recognize which ego functions are disturbed, in what ways they have been affected, and how the disturbances in question are related to inner conflict: in particular, what is being warded off and what is the anxiety, that is, the frightening fantasy, connected with it.

We may summarize the psychopathological characteristics of the psychoses which differentiate them from the neuroses as follows: (1) a greater degree of instinctual regression or infantilism; (2) a greater prominence of manifestations of the instinctual drive of aggression and of conflicts over such manifestations; and (3) more severe and more widespread abnormalities in various ego and superego functions. These last are generally motivated by a need to prevent the emergence of anxiety in a situation of inner conflict, i.e., they serve a defensive function primarily. Such defensive alterations in ego and superego functions play a major role in the clinical symptoms that characterize the psychoses. Thus, for example, they appear to be of decisive importance in the appearance of the subjective and behavioral symptoms which Freud called the break with reality and which he considered to be the most important single characteristic of the psychoses.

Let us attempt now to illustrate both the validity and the explanatory value of the statements just given concerning the psychopathology of the psychoses. Is it really possible to explain the clinical features of the psychoses more satisfactorily with the help of these ideas, which derive from the structural theory? Are they superior to the familiar concepts of a primary phase of libidinal decathexis and narcissistic regression and a secondary, restitutive phase of recathexis?

In our discussion we shall direct principal attention to the topic of defensive alterations of ego and superego functions. It does not appear to be necessary to call particular attention, at the present time, to the characteristic features of the *instinctual* lives of psychotic patients. In the first place, there is general agreement on this score among psychoanalysts. In the second place, there is already a voluminous literature both on pregenitality in psychotic patients and on the importance of the role in their mental lives of derivatives of the aggressive drive.

We may begin with the following clinical example. A psychotic patient, who was in conflict over her angry, sadistic impulses toward her husband, defended herself against those impulses by going into a trance or stuporous state in which she neither moved, nor spoke, nor thought. She behaved as though she must tie herself hand and foot, and even tongue and brain, lest she burst forth in a fury and destroy and devour the object of her wrath. A neurotic patient's defense against similar impulses would ordinarily disrupt her relationship to her environment much less than does falling into a stupor. She might develop the hysterical symptom of nausea, for example, or a stomachache. Such a symptom would be disturbing to the patient herself, but it would not affect her behavior in a way as obvious to those about her as was the case with the patient who became stuporous. We may

say that in our psychotic patient there was a defensively motivated disruption of certain ego functions which are, ordinarily, considerably less affected by inner conflict in normal or
neurotic individuals: voluntary motility, external sensory
perception, and conscious thought. This disruption resulted
in a severe though temporary withdrawal from external
reality.

Since one of the questions in which we are particularly
interested is whether the proposed revisions in theory are of
any value in the treatment of psychotic patients, we may
make the following observation at this point. According to
Freud's original theory, this patient's stupor would be viewed
as the consequence of psychotic repression, i.e., of a decathexis of external object representations. If one accepts this
explanation of the facts, then when one is treating the patient
one's interpretation to her will be essentially along this line.
One will say, in effect, "When you can't express your anger
directly, you lose interest in everything about you. You turn
away from the world." This is as far as one can go on the
basis of Freud's earlier formulations. However, by revising
those formulations as suggested here, by applying to the psychoses what Freud has demonstrated concerning anxiety and
defense in the neuroses, it was possible to go much farther
with the patient. One could say to her, in effect, "The fact
that you have to paralyze your mind and body so completely
when you're angry at your husband indicates that you're very
afraid of becoming openly angry at him. You seem to be
afraid of what you'd think, and of what you'd do. It's important to try to find out what wishes or ideas you're so afraid
of, and why they frighten you so, i.e., what you think will
happen if you think or wish them." Analyst and patient were
thus led to explore the motives of the patient's defense as

well as its historical (infantile) determinants. The revision in theory made possible an advance in technique.

In the case just cited the conflict which resulted in the patient's total withdrawal from her environment was an unconscious one. The patient was aware only of its result. This is not necessarily the case. For example, a single woman in her thirties was brought to a mental hospital by the police because she had barricaded herself in her room and had refused to come out. In the hospital she was calm, cooperative, and communicative. She explained that she had locked herself in lest she kill her parents, in whose home she still lived. In this case the patient's motive for breaking off contact with her environment was a conscious one. She withdrew in order to defend herself against the temptation to kill her parents, a temptation which terrified her.[5]

We see therefore how defensive alterations in ego functions can give rise to a break with reality. In the two cases above, each patient withdrew from contact with persons in her environment in order to defend herself against instinctual wishes toward those persons. Incidentally, it must not be assumed that only murderous or sadistic wishes can result in such withdrawal. Patients may employ similar defenses, with similar results, against instinctual wishes in which libidinal elements play a more obvious or predominant role. What is important to note is that there are patients who defend themselves against frightening instinctual impulses by alterations of various ego functions which result in a disruption of their relations with their environment. It is not necessary to explain the disruption of object relations, the break with reality, as Freud called it, by the theoretical assumption that a libidinal decathexis has occurred. On the contrary, the

[5] We are indebted to Dr. B. D. Bandler for this case material.

explanation offered here, of a defensive disruption of ego functions, is superior on two counts. First, it fits the clinical data better. Second, it is consonant with Freud's later, structural theory of the mind, the theory which is our basic conceptual tool for the understanding of mental phenomena in general.

Many types of defensive alteration of ego functions other than the ones just illustrated may also result in disturbances or even in disruption of the patient's relationship to his environment. For example, it seems very common, at least in mildly psychotic individuals, for disturbances in the ego's integrative capacity to produce such a result. Patients of this sort, like children, are unable to make any sort of sensible, causal connection between what is happening in their lives now and what happened a few minutes or hours before. Inner and outer events are isolated to a surprising degree. In severe cases, the patient has no feeling whatever of sense or continuity to his life or thoughts. Everything is bewildering and confusing. In addition to the subjective disturbances just mentioned, there may be equally obvious objective ones. The patient may be openly sexual in his behavior at one moment and violently self-punitive a moment later, with no sign of integration between superego and instinctual demands of the sort which the ego normally is able to effect once it has developed beyond its earliest stages.

It may be remarked at this point that the disturbance which patients of this sort show in their relationship to reality cannot be satisfactorily explained by assuming a decathexis of external objects. These patients show evidence that the mental representations of external objects have never ceased to be strongly cathected; indeed, they are often quite obviously intensely fixated on the original objects of childhood, on parents and siblings, during their entire lives. The clinical features which they present seem to constitute a clear contradiction of the assumption that psychotic states are initiated by a process of decathexis of the mental representation of external objects. In order to explain satisfactorily the clinical features which these patients show, it seems that one must abandon that assumption in favor of the revisions concerning conflict, anxiety, and defense in psychosis which are here suggested.

In the patients of this sort whom we have been able to study, i.e., in those seen in office practice, such gross disturbances of the ego function of integration as have just been described, appear to serve a defensive function. The disruption of continuity of mental life is unconsciously produced in order to avoid an intolerable sense of anxiety or guilt. Thus, we may say that in cases of this sort inner mental conflict has caused a regressive impairment of the ego's capacity for integration of such a degree that the patients in question, like very small children, are unable to understand either what is happening to them or within themselves and are, likewise, unable to act other than impulsively. When the disturbance of the ego's integrative capacity is widespread, it may be difficult, indeed, to detect the mental conflicts which underlie it and which have given rise to it. In less severe cases, the conflicts are more easily discernible. For example, one patient could not understand why the very people whom she loved most were so often unkind to her or even quarreled openly with her. The answer to this puzzling question began to be apparent only after the following bit of her behavior during her analytic sessions was correctly understood. There were times, when, during an hour, she shouted at the analyst, obviously in anger. If the analyst said nothing, she would appear to suppress her anger and go on talking in a normal conversational tone of voice. On one occasion, the analyst remarked, after she had resumed her normal, conversational tone, that she must be angry at him. She denied being so, as patients often do when such a possibility is raised with them; but, what is more important, she had no idea why the analyst should have imagined that she might be angry. Further discussion revealed that she was unaware that she was shouting even while she was doing so. The motor act which expressed her anger as well as the proprioceptive and auditory sensations connected with it were unintegrated by her ego. On the contrary, they were actively isolated by it. One can now readily understand at least part of the reason why this patient was often unkindly treated by those whom she loved. She fought with them, sometimes violently, without being aware that what she was doing was, in fact, fighting. It took many months of analysis to discover the motive for the defensive impairment of her ego's integrative capacity during moments of anger. Her unconscious castrative and cannibalistic, murderous wishes gave rise to guilt feelings which were so intense as to make her feel that she would be better off dead and that she should kill herself. By being unaware of yelling and fighting, she could avoid, or at least could mitigate, the associated guilt and self-destructive tendencies.

Here then is an example of disturbed object relations resulting from a disturbance of the ego's integrative function which had primarily a defensive purpose. In another patient one of the defenses against frightening wishes was of still another, though closely related sort. In this patient, who was a man, the wish to be loved as a woman aroused intolerable castration anxiety. One of his ways of defending himself against such wishes was to become confused and disorganized in his ability to think and to be unable to understand what was said to him, particularly during an analytic session. In his case, the defensive impairment of ego function under these circumstances sometimes went so far that he could not even understand the meaning of simple words; i.e., his inner conflict resulted in an impairment of language, one of the ego's most important and oldest functions. The inevitable disturbance of object relations which resulted from this patient's impairment of thought and language is obvious.

It seems necessary to mention the following considerations at this point in connection with the two cases just mentioned. These considerations are somewhat aside from our main interest at the moment, but they are of such practical importance that they should not be passed by. In both of the examples just cited, one can observe that the regressive disturbance of ego functions served more than purely defensive ends. In the first case, it clearly served to facilitate the expression of anger as well, i.e., it served in part an instinctual end. In addition, it was, at times, a way in which the patient provoked people to mistreat her, i.e., it served her superego's aims, namely, the need to be punished as well. In the second case, the patient's confusion, particularly in the analytic situation, was a mute plea to his analyst to help him, i.e., it expressed an instinctual wish as well as serving as a defense against that wish.

The concept of multiple function (Waelder, 1930) and its place in the conceptual framework of the structural theory has been discussed at some length in Chapter 9. The practical importance of bearing that concept in mind is particularly great when one is attempting to treat psychotic patients psychotherapeutically. It is commonplace that in neuroses, and particularly in such character disturbances as addictions and perversions, the degree of gratification inherent in the illness or in a particular symptom may be so great as to render attempts at cure by analysis very difficult or even impossible. The same thing may be true in psychotic patients, and often to an even greater degree. Much of the behavior of psychotic patients, and much of their inner mental lives as well, obviously serves to gratify infantile instinctual wishes as well as to prevent the development of anxiety or guilt. In assessing the accessibility of a psychotic patient to treatment, and in deciding how he may best be treated, one must attempt to understand correctly the interplay of forces within the patient's mind. Moreover, the relative importance of those forces may change, particularly during the course of analysis, and it is of the utmost importance to recognize such changes and to take account of them in one's therapeutic work with the patient. In the present imperfect state of our knowledge, the best efforts and the most careful attempts at assessment may prove to be inadequate. It seems likely, however, that one will be successful more often if one brings to the task as accurate an understanding of the psychopathology of the psychoses as it has thus far been possible to formulate.

Let us turn now to a consideration of those cataclysmic disturbances in object relations to which we refer as delusions of world destruction. They are common in psychotic patients and they represent a severe degree of disturbance in a patient's relation to his environment. It will be recalled that Freud (1911b, 1914a) proposed to explain delusions of world destruction on what are essentially economic or quantitative grounds. A patient with such a delusion, said Freud, has withdrawn his libidinal cathexes from most or all of the mental representations of the objects in the world about him as a consequence of his illness. The endopsychic perception of this libidinal decathexis, its consequence for the patient's relationship to the outer world, is that the world seems profoundly changed, unreal, or even destroyed and dead. In other words, a psychotic patient's delusion that the

[166]

world has been destroyed is to be explained as a direct and simple consequence of libidinal decathexis.

Such is the psychopathology of delusions of world destruction according to Freud's original theory. What have we to offer in its place which will be more consonant with the structural theory, and perhaps also more consonant with the observable clinical phenomena?

Our explanation must be a tentative one, since unfortunately it is not based on the actual analysis of patients who exhibited such delusions. What we suggest probably happens in such patients is this. A patient who is violently angry wishes to destroy and smash everything about him. The guilt and anxiety that would arise were he to become aware of his wish and to acknowledge it as his own are too great for him to bear. Instead he becomes convinced that the world has indeed been destroyed, though not through any fault of his own. It is either God who has done it, or natural forces, or communists, criminals, etc. We should explain this symptom, then, by saying that, along with other defensive activities of the ego (e.g., projection) which serve the purpose of avoiding the anxiety associated with his destructive wishes, the patient's ability to distinguish external reality from fantasy has been seriously impaired (regressively altered) with the result that a somewhat distorted, wish-fulfilling fantasy is perceived as real. We must add that in many cases, despite the defensive impairment of reality testing and the other, accompanying defenses, a considerable degree of anxiety and guilt nevertheless develop. This was something which Freud recognized as a clinical fact, and to which he alluded in his paper on "The Loss of Reality in Neurosis and Psychosis" (1924b), but which he found very difficult to explain on the basis of his theory of libidinal decathexis. If one replaces this theory by the one suggested here, it is a clinical fact

[167]

which falls readily into line with what we know about similar phenomena in the neuroses, namely, that in symptom formation defenses do not always suffice to prevent the development of anxiety. At times the best they can do is to diminish it to a greater or lesser degree.

This explanation of the psychopathology of delusions of world destruction is perhaps more complicated than Freud's original explanation. Nevertheless, it appears to us to be closer to the clinical facts as well as more consonant with the structural theory. It explains more of what we can actually observe in patients as well as explaining what we can observe in terms of mental processes which we know are important in mental life in general. Thus, as we have noted, it explains why many patients with delusions of world destruction are terrified, which Freud's original theory cannot satisfactorily do. In addition, it permits us to understand the relationship between delusions of world destruction and another common type of delusion in psychotic patients, a type which is closely related to world-destruction delusions. There are many psychotic patients with messianic delusions. They believe that the world has come to an end, or that it is about to do so, and that it is their mission to rescue it. Equally frequent are delusions that danger threatens a particular person whom the patient is concerned to rescue.

The explanation which we have offered as to the psychopathology of delusions of world destruction makes it easy to understand the clinically observable relationship between such delusions and messianic ones. One need only assume that in the case of the messianic patient, the patient's own role has changed from that of a mere observer of the destruction about him to that of an active savior, rescuer, or restorer of life and health to those threatened by the destructive forces which seem to him to be raging everywhere. Thus we

[168]

would say that the patient with a delusion of world destruction has attempted to defend himself against his own aggressive or sadistic impulses, at least in part, by a regressive disturbance of the ego function of reality testing, whereas the messianic patient exhibits both a disturbance of reality testing and a reaction formation against his frightening impulses, or an attempt to undo them as well.

In the last several pages we have tried to show that various disturbances of the psychotic patient's relationship to his environment can be explained without recourse to the concept of libidinal decathexis of object representations. Such disturbances are more satisfactorily explained with the help of Freud's later concepts, in particular the concepts of the structural theory. The break with reality, which, it will be recalled, Freud considered to be the most essential single characteristic of the psychoses, is best explained by the concept of defensive alterations of ego function.

We propose to turn now to a similar examination of the other symptoms of the psychoses which Freud considered to be of major importance: megalomania, hypochondriacal symptoms, delusions (other than those of world destruction and of bodily change), and hallucinations. In each instance we shall compare the validity of the theory of the psychopathology of the psychoses which we have suggested here with Freud's original theory. The reader will recall that in his original theory, which is still generally accepted as far as these basic fundamentals are concerned, Freud explained the initial break with reality, megalomania, and hypochondriasis as due to the withdrawal of libido from object representations and its transformation into narcissistic libido, while he explained delusions and hallucinations as phenomena of a secondary, restitutive phase.

Let us begin with the symptom of megalomania. Our first

remark will be a purely clinical one. It is true that megalomania is a frequent symptom in schizophrenia. It is not a universal one, however. Many psychotic patients have an abnormally low self-esteem and very great feelings of either worthlessness, impotence, or both. Even though such patients are self-centered, perhaps in the same way in which a child is self-centered, they are neither megalomanic nor self-loving. These are clinical facts which are difficult to explain if one follows the assumption which Freud first made in the paper on Schreber, that every psychosis is initiated by a shift of cathexis from object representations to the self, i.e., by a transformation of object libido into narcissistic libido. If such a shift, such a transformation, is indeed the essential and fateful first step in the psychotic process, then every psychotic patient should have at least a phase of megalomania. If one explains psychoses on this basis, one is at a loss to understand why it should be that some patients suffer from what appears to be exactly the reverse of megalomania, i.e., from feelings of worthlessness or of being nonentities altogether. It would seem to be more logical to assume that in such patients narcissistic libido has been pathologically depleted rather than pathologically increased.

However, these are not the only difficulties encountered in using Freud's original theory. A closer scrutiny of the clinical facts concerning megalomania in psychosis reveals additional difficulties. For example, when one is able to study megalomanic delusions in patients in detail one discovers that in many cases such delusions have a primarily defensive function. They serve to prevent the development of anxiety, anxiety which would otherwise be aroused by the patient's libidinal and aggressive wishes. In such cases it is as though the patient is saying to himself, "It isn't true that I'm helpless and would perish without my mother, or father, or both. I'm omnipotent. I can do anything I want, I'm so big and power-ful." Cases of this sort resemble the children described by A. Freud (1936) who deny, with the help of wish-fulfilling fantasies, that they are small, weak, and dependent on their parents. If we follow her terminology in describing what happens in a psychotic patient of this kind, we should say that the patient has defended himself against the emergence of anxiety about being weak, helpless, or castrated (1) by a wish-fulfilling fantasy of omnipotence or grandeur, and (2) by a disturbance, or regressive alteration, of the ego function of reality testing. The result of these defensive reactions is the clinical symptom of megalomania, that is, a grandiose delusion. Moreover, we can understand that if the defenses just described are not wholly successful, the patient will show a mixture of ideas of grandiosity and inadequacy, as indeed many patients do. Finally, there are patients with terrifying fears of helplessness in whom the particular defense of wish-fulfilling, omnipotent fantasies does not appear. These are patients in whom we may find clinically no signs of megalomania, but rather ideas of inadequacy or even of nonentity, together with more or less intense conscious anxi-ety, the amount of anxiety being dependent on how success-ful other defenses have been.

It would seem, therefore, that although the explanation offered by Freud (1911b) in the paper on Schreber for the clinical phenomenon of megalomania in psychosis is a far simpler one than that which is based on the structural theory, it is one which is inadequate to explain the clinical facts as we observe them and study them in the patients whom we treat. The facts as we know them can be explained more adequately and more precisely with the help of Freud's later contributions to psychoanalysis: the structural theory and the revised theory of anxiety and defense which is, properly considered, a part of the structural theory.

It will be recalled that Freud's original theory assumes hypochondriacal symptoms to be the third major symptomatic consequence of the regressive phase of psychoses. The break with reality is assumed to be the consequence of a withdrawal of object cathexes; megalomania and hypochondriasis are assumed to result from the transformation of the withdrawn object libido into narcissistic libido. Moreover, as noted earlier, hypochondriasis was equated with what Freud called anxiety neurosis proper (1895b, 1914a), one of the actual neuroses. In both conditions the excessive amounts of undischarged libido were assumed to be transformed into anxiety. Thus hypochondriasis was assumed to consist in a hypercathexis of one or more body organs with narcissistic libido. The libidinal hypercathexis was assumed to account for the patient's excessive preoccupation with and interest in his body and its functioning. The clinically observable anxiety, on the other hand, was attributed to the transformation of the excessive libidinal cathexes directly into anxiety. It may be noted that, prior to 1926, the assumption that neurotic anxiety was transformed, undischarged (dammed-up) libido was an integral part of psychoanalytic theory. It was not until that date (1926) that Freud abandoned that theory in favor of the current theory of anxiety as a signal of danger and a motive for repression and other defenses.

How can the clinical phenomena of hypochondriasis in the psychoses be explained within the conceptual framework of the structural theory, with its corollary of the signal function of anxiety?

On the basis of our experience with hypochondriacal symptoms in psychotic patients we would suggest that the psychodynamics of such symptoms are the same in every essential respect as those which underlie the conversion symptoms of hysterical patients. Like hysterical conversion symptoms, the symptoms of hypochondriasis are the expression in body language of a fantasy which is itself a compromise between an instinctual wish which has given rise to anxiety and conflict, and the defense against that wish (Bak, 1954; Eissler, 1953; Waelder, 1951; Katan, 1954; Róheim, 1955; Arlow, 1949; Wexler, 1951; Schmideberg, 1951; Searles, 1962). Even the disturbance in reality testing is very similar in the two conditions. Hysterical patients, like psychotic ones, are often firmly convinced that their symptoms are due to objective physical disease. To convince them that their symptoms are psychogenic, that they are caused by inner conflict rather than by an ulcer, or cancer, or infection, may be difficult or impossible.

The descriptive, clinical differences between conversion symptoms in psychotic patients and in neurotic ones appear to be explainable, at least in large part, in terms of greater variation in the degree of disturbance of ego functions in the psychoses (Hartmann, 1953). For example, a psychotic patient may defend himself against anal sexual wishes by a complete denial that that part of his body exists. Such a patient develops the hypochondriacal symptom that he has no anus. Another psychotic patient may complain that a bone is stuck in his throat. Here the defensive distortion of his fellatio fantasy is limited to displacement or symbolization: it is not a penis, it is a bone. Still another psychotic patient, who was in conflict over oral-sadistic impulses, reported a feeling that his teeth had suddenly grown larger. In this case, as in the previous one, the compromise between wish and defense is particularly clear. What we wish to emphasize, however, is that in all such cases the symptom is the bodily expression of a fantasy, a fantasy which results from a conflict over an instinctual wish. The wish gives rise to anxiety, the anxiety to defensive reactions, and to an eventual compromise, just as happens in the psychoneuroses. If the defenses are relatively successful, little or no anxiety will accompany the symptom which results. If the defenses are relatively unsuccessful, the symptom will be accompanied by much anxiety.

This last point is one that is particularly important to bear in mind in one's actual, clinical work with patients. It is relevant not only in dealing with hypochondriacal symptoms, but in dealing with all symptoms in any patient, whether neurotic or psychotic. In the case of any symptom which is accompanied by anxiety, analytic investigation will show that the anxiety is due to the individual's reaction to an instinctual wish against which he could defend himself with only partial success. It is erroneous to assume, as is sometimes done, that anxiety is a consequence of symptom formation rather than the initiator of the defensive efforts which are part of the dynamics of symptom formation (cf. Arlow, 1959).

To return to the problems raised by hypochondriacal symptoms, we believe that, like the other symptoms of the psychoses, hypochondriacal symptoms are not properly explainable as the result of libidinal regression and displacement. Like megalomania and the break with reality, they are more satisfactorily explained in terms of the conceptual framework of the structural theory, with its emphasis on anxiety, conflict, and defense.

Let us turn now to the symptoms of the psychoses which Freud originally attributed to a secondary, restitutive phase of the illness. These symptoms are hallucinations and delusions.[6] They are assumed to result from a process of partial and pathological recathexis of object representations. In particular, this recathexis is assumed to be limited to the object representations in the system *Pcs.*, i.e., to the word representations, as distinct from the nonverbal object representations, which Freud (1915b) proposed to assign to the system *Ucs.* We suggest that delusions and hallucinations may be explained as follows within the conceptual framework of the structural theory. In either case a fantasy has resulted from the patient's inner conflict, whether that conflict is over instinctual wishes, self-punitive demands, or both. Whatever other defensive mechanisms may be involved in the formation of the fantasy, e.g., repression, projection, denial, etc., there is among the ego's defenses a regressive alteration of reality testing. The ego's ability to distinguish between external reality and the particular fantasy in question is impaired in order to avoid or minimize the development of anxiety. Thus the fantasy appears real to the patient. Instead of being experienced as a daydream, it is experienced as a delusion or a hallucination. What determines whether it is the one or the other is the presence or absence of sensory elements in the fantasy. If there are such elements, the result is a hallucination. If there are none, it is a delusion.

[6] It should be noted that Freud's early theory is not quite consistent on this point. Delusions of world destruction, hypochondriacal delusions, and megalomania are delusional, perhaps at times hallucinatory, symptoms of the regressive phase of a psychosis. They are assumed to be direct results of the narcissistic, regressive disturbances of the patient's libidinal economy. All other delusions and hallucinations are assumed to be symptoms of the restitutive phase of a psychosis. In his last published discussion of delusions and hallucinations, which was unfortunately a brief one, Freud (1938, sec. iii) suggested that the psychodynamics of such symptoms may be the resultant of the forces involved in intrapsychic conflict, just as a manifest dream is. This view comes very close to the one we propose. It differs only in that Freud apparently retained his original thesis that the initial phase of psychosis is one of decathexis of object representations.

For example, a normal individual whose mother has died may at times wish that she could hear once more her mother's voice telling her, "I love you." A psychotic patient heard instead her mother's voice repeat the words. In her case the anxiety and guilt feelings associated with her highly ambivalent attitude toward her mother produced an alteration of her ability to test reality which resulted in an actual hallucination.

A male patient defended himself against unconscious sexual wishes involving his analyst by projecting onto his wife the wish for sexual relations with a man. At times during his analysis, this projection appeared as part of the manifest content of his dreams. At other times, however, he was convinced of his wife's flirtatiousness even when he was awake. At such times his ability to distinguish between external reality and his own fantasy was impaired by his inner conflict to such a degree that even during waking hours his fantasy was real to him.

In this case, the primarily defensive nature of the disturbance of reality testing is very clear. It may be remarked in passing, however, that the patient's diminished ability to test reality was not exclusively defensive. It served a multiple function. In addition to its defensive function, it led to outbursts of rage and destructiveness. In other words, it facilitated the discharge of certain instinctual elements, largely sadistic in nature, as well as fulfilling the function of defense.

Thus delusions and hallucinations, like dreams, can be understood as the result of a more or less complex interplay among id, ego, and superego. In the psychotic patient, as in the dreamer, a regressive alteration of the ego function of reality testing leads the individual himself to consider as a part of external reality the result of his own, inner mental processes. In the dreamer it is the state of sleep which has

[176]

produced a disturbance of reality testing. In the psychotic patient, reality testing has been altered as part of the ego's defensive effort to avoid the emergence of anxiety.

It may be added that this explanation of the psychopathology of psychotic delusions and hallucinations does away with the necessity of explaining delusions of world destruction, hypochondriacal delusions, and megalomania on a different basis from all other delusions and hallucinations. The conceptual framework of the structural theory, applied as we have attempted to do, permits one to explain all delusions and hallucinations on the same psychopathological basis.

One final remark may be in order concerning the theory we have advanced of the psychopathology of the psychoses in general. It will be recalled that Freud's basic attitude to the psychoses was that they show a fundamental unity with the neuroses as far as their psychopathology is concerned. The correctness of that basic attitude appears to us to be amply substantiated both by the work of Freud himself and by that of other psychoanalysts who have followed him. What we have done is to apply the basic attitude that neurosis and psychosis are psychologically similar in an even more far-reaching way than Freud was able to do in 1911. Before he evolved the structural theory Freud found it necessary to postulate that repression in the psychoses is a different process from repression in the neuroses. In the psychoses, said Freud, what we call repression is pathological in and of itself. It results directly in the appearance of symptoms. In the neuroses, on the other hand, repression is not the pathological event. It only sets the stage for what may or may not happen subsequently, namely, a failure of repression, with the emergence of symptoms. In other words, repression is itself a normal phenomenon. It is when repression fails that neurosis begins.

We hope we have shown that, with the help of the structural theory, it is possible to subsume the psychopathology of the psychoses under the same general scheme that Freud himself and others have applied so successfully to neurotic and to many normal mental phenomena. If we have been successful, it follows that there is no more a sharp line of division between what is to be called psychotic and what we call neurotic than there is between the neurotic and the normal. Each shades off into the other just as do the colors of a continuous spectrum. Psychotic and neurotic may be useful classificatory concepts in a very general and imprecise way. They are what one might call rough and ready terms. Any satisfactory classification, however, if it is to be a psychopathological one, must be formulated in terms of the nature of the patient's conflicts and, above all, in terms of the integrity or degree of disturbance of his various ego functions.

Bibliography

ABRAHAM, K. (1924), A Short Study of the Development of the Libido Viewed in the Light of Mental Disorders. *Selected Papers on Psycho-Analysis.* London: Hogarth Press, 1942, pp. 418-502.

ALEXANDER, F. (1930), *The Psychoanalysis of the Total Personality.* New York & Washington: Nervous and Mental Disease Publishing Co.

ARLOW, J. A. (1949), Anal Sensations and Feelings of Persecution. *Psychoanal. Quart.,* 18:79-84.

―― (1952), A Creative Spell Simulating Orgasm. Paper read before the New York Psychoanalytic Society.

―― (1953), Masturbation and Symptom Formation. *J. Amer. Psychoanal. Assn.,* 1:45-58.

―― (1956), *The Legacy of Sigmund Freud.* New York: International Universities Press.

―― (1957), A Contribution to the Psychology of Time. Paper read at the Los Angeles Psychoanalytic Society.

―― (1959), The Structure of the *Déjà Vu* Experience. *J. Amer. Psychoanal. Assn.,* 7:611-631.

―― (1961), Silence and the Theory of Technique. *J. Amer. Psychoanal. Assn.,* 9:44-55.

―― (1963), Conflict, Regression, and Symptom Formation. *Int. J. Psycho-Anal.,* 44:12-22.

BAK, R. (1939), Regression of Ego-Orientation and Libido in Schizophrenia. *Int. J. Psycho-Anal.,* 20:64-71.

―― (1954), The Schizophrenic Defence against Aggression. *Int. J. Psycho-Anal.,* 35:129-133.

BERES, D. (1956), Ego Deviation and the Concept of Schizophrenia. *The Psychoanalytic Study of the Child,* 12:164-235. New York: International Universities Press.

—— & Obers, S. J. (1950), The Effects of Extreme Deprivation in Infancy on Psychic Structure in Adolescence: A Study in Ego Development. *The Psychoanalytic Study of the Child,* 5:212-235. New York: International Universities Press.

Bernfeld, S. (1944), Freud's Earliest Theories and the School of Helmholtz. *Psychoanal. Quart.,* 13:341-362.

Bonaparte, M. (1952), Some Biopsychical Aspects of Sado-Masochism. *Int. J. Psycho-Anal.,* 33:373-384.

Brenner, C. (1955a), *An Elementary Textbook of Psychoanalysis.* New York: International Universities Press.

—— (1955b), Theory of Parapraxes. *Bull. Phila. Assn. Psychoanal.,* 5:110-113.

—— (1957), The Nature and Development of the Concept of Repression in Freud's Writings. *The Psychoanalytic Study of the Child,* 12:19-46. New York: International Universities Press.

Daly, C. D. (1943), The Role of Menstruation in Human Phylogenesis and Ontogenesis. *Int. J. Psycho-Anal.,* 24:151-170.

Eidelberg, L. (1936), A Contribution to the Study of Slips of the Tongue. *Studies in Psychoanalysis.* New York: International Universities Press, 1952, pp. 154-161.

—— (1944), A Further Contribution to the Study of Slips of the Tongue. *Studies in Psychoanalysis.* New York: International Universities Press, 1952, pp. 162-173.

Eissler, K. R. (1953), Notes Upon the Emotionality of a Schizophrenic Patient and Its Relation to Problems of Technique. *The Psychoanalytic Study of the Child,* 8:199-251. New York: International Universities Press.

—— (1962), On the Metapsychology of the Preconscious: A Tentative Contribution to Psychoanalytic Morphology. *The Psychoanalytic Study of the Child,* 17:9-41. New York: International Universities Press.

Fenichel, O. (1939), *Problems of Psychoanalytic Technique.* New York: Psychoanalytic Quarterly, 1941.

—— (1945), *The Psychoanalytic Theory of Neurosis.* New York: Norton.

Ferenczi, S. (1913), Stages in the Development of the Sense of Reality. *Sex in Psychoanalysis.* New York: Basic Books, 1950, 213-239.

—— (1924), *Thalassa: A Theory of Genitality.* New York: Psychoanalytic Quarterly, 1938.

Fisher, C. (1954), Dreams and Perception: The Role of Preconscious and Primary Modes of Perception in Dream Formation. *J. Amer. Psychoanal. Assn.,* 2:389-445.

—— (1957), A Study of the Preliminary Stages of the Construction of Dreams and Images. *J. Amer. Psychoanal. Assn.,* 5:5-60.

—— & DEMENT, W. C. (1963), On Dream Deprivation. Paper read before the New York Psychoanalytic Society.

—— & PAUL, I. H. (1959), The Effect of Subliminal Visual Stimulation on Images and Dreams: A Validation Study. *J. Amer. Psychoanal. Assn.*, 7:35-83.

FREUD, A. (1936), *The Ego and the Mechanisms of Defense.* New York: International Universities Press, 1946.

—— (1951), Observations on Child Development. *The Psychoanalytic Study of the Child,* 6:18-30. New York: International Universities Press.

—— (1963), Regression as a Principle in Mental Development. *Bull. Menninger Clin.,* 27:126-139.

FREUD, S. (1891), *On Aphasia.* New York: International Universities Press, 1953.

—— (1895a), Project for a Scientific Psychology. *The Origins of Psychoanalysis: Letters to Wilhelm Fliess, Drafts and Notes: 1887-1902.* New York: Basic Books, 1954.

—— (1895b) On the Grounds for Detaching a Particular Syndrome from Neurasthenia under the Description 'Anxiety Neurosis.' *Standard Edition,* 3:87-120. London: Hogarth Press, 1962.

—— (1896), Further Remarks on the Neuro-Psychoses of Defence. *Standard Edition,* 3:159-188. London: Hogarth Press, 1962.

—— (1900), The Interpretation of Dreams. *Standard Edition,* 4 & 5. London: Hogarth Press, 1953.

—— (1901), The Psychopathology of Everyday Life. *Standard Edition,* 6:1-279. London: Hogarth Press, 1960.

—— (1905), Three Essays on the Theory of Sexuality. *Standard Edition,* 7:122-243. London: Hogarth Press, 1953.

—— (1908), Hysterical Phantasies and Their Relation to Bisexuality. *Standard Edition,* 9:155-166. London: Hogarth Press, 1959.

—— (1909), Analysis of a Phobia in a Five-year-old Boy. *Standard Edition,* 10:3-149. London: Hogarth Press, 1955.

—— (1911a), Formulations on the Two Principles of Mental Functioning. *Standard Edition,* 12:213-226. London: Hogarth Press, 1958.

—— (1911b), Psycho-Analytic Notes on an Autobiographical Account of a Case of Paranoia. *Standard Edition,* 12:3-84. London: Hogarth Press, 1958.

—— (1913a), The Disposition to Obsessional Neurosis. *Standard Edition,* 12:311-326. London: Hogarth Press, 1958.

—— (1913b), Totem and Taboo. *Standard Edition,* 13:1-161. London: Hogarth Press, 1955.

—— (1914a), On Narcissism: An Introduction. *Standard Edition,* 14:67-104. London: Hogarth Press, 1957.

[181]

—— (1914b), On the History of the Psycho-Analytic Movement. *Standard Edition*, 14:7-66. London: Hogarth Press, 1957.

—— (1915a), Repression. *Standard Edition*, 14:141-158. London: Hogarth Press, 1957.

—— (1915b), The Unconscious. *Standard Edition*, 14:159-215. London: Hogarth Press, 1957.

—— (1915c), Thoughts for the Times on War and Death. *Standard Edition*, 14:273-302. London: Hogarth Press, 1957.

—— (1916-1917), Introductory Lectures on Psycho-Analysis. *Standard Edition*, 15 & 16. London: Hogarth Press, 1963.

—— (1917a), A Metapsychological Supplement to the Theory of Dreams. *Standard Edition*, 14:217-236. London: Hogarth Press, 1957.

—— (1917b), Mourning and Melancholia. *Standard Edition*, 14:237-258. London: Hogarth Press, 1957.

—— (1917c), On Transformations of Instinct as Exemplified in Anal Erotism. *Standard Edition*, 17:126-133. London: Hogarth Press, 1955.

—— (1920), Beyond the Pleasure Principle. *Standard Edition*, 18:3-66. London: Hogarth Press, 1955.

—— (1921), Group Psychology and the Analysis of the Ego. *Standard Edition*, 18:67-144. London: Hogarth Press, 1955.

—— (1923a), The Ego and the Id. *Standard Edition*, 19:3-68. London: Hogarth Press, 1961.

—— (1923b), Remarks on the Theory and Practice of Dream-Interpretation. *Standard Edition*, 19:108-121. London: Hogarth Press, 1961.

—— (1924a), Neurosis and Psychosis. *Standard Edition*, 19:149-156. London: Hogarth Press, 1961.

—— (1924b), The Loss of Reality in Neurosis and Psychosis. *Standard Edition*, 19:183-190. London: Hogarth Press, 1961.

—— (1924c), A Short Account of Psycho-Analysis. *Standard Edition*, 19:191-212. London: Hogarth Press, 1961.

—— (1926), Inhibitions, Symptoms and Anxiety. *Standard Edition*, 20:77-178. London: Hogarth Press, 1959.

—— (1932a), *New Introductory Lectures*. New York: Norton, 1933.

—— (1932b), Why War? *Collected Papers*, 5:273-287. London: Hogarth Press.

—— (1936), A Disturbance of Memory on the Acropolis. *Collected Papers*, 5:302-312. London: Hogarth Press, 1950.

—— (1937-1939), *Moses and Monotheism*. London: Hogarth Press.

—— (1938), Constructions in Analysis. *Collected Papers*, 5:358-371. London: Hogarth Press, 1950.

—— (1940), *An Outline of Psychoanalysis*. New York: Norton, 1949.

GILL, M. M. (1963), *Topography and Systems in Psychoanalytic Theory* [*Psychological Issues*, Monograph 10]. New York: International Universities Press.

HARTMANN, H. (1939a), *Ego Psychology and the Problem of Adaptation.* New York: International Universities Press, 1958.

—— (1939b), Psycho-Analysis and the Concept of Health. *Int. J. Psycho-Anal.*, 20:308-321.

—— (1948), Comments on the Psychoanalytic Theory of Instinctual Drives. *Psychoanal. Quart.*, 17:368-388.

—— (1950a), Psychoanalysis and Developmental Psychology. *The Psychoanalytic Study of the Child*, 5:7-17. New York: International Universities Press.

—— (1950b), Comments on the Psychoanalytic Theory of the Ego. *The Psychoanalytic Study of the Child*, 5:74-96. New York: International Universities Press.

—— (1951), Technical Implications of Ego Psychology. *Psychoanal. Quart.*, 20:31-43.

—— (1953), Contribution to the Metapsychology of Schizophrenia. *The Psychoanalytic Study of the Child*, 8:177-198. New York: International Universities Press.

—— (1956), The Development of the Ego Concept in Freud's Work. *Int. J. Psycho-Anal.*, 37:425-438.

—— (1958), Comments on the Scientific Aspects of Psychoanalysis. *The Psychoanalytic Study of the Child*, 13:127-146. New York: International Universities Press.

—— & KRIS, E. (1945), The Genetic Approach in Psychoanalysis. *The Psychoanalytic Study of the Child*, 1:11-30. New York: International Universities Press.

—— —— & LOEWENSTEIN, R. M. (1946), Comments on the Formation of Psychic Structure. *The Psychoanalytic Study of the Child*, 2:11-38. New York: International Universities Press.

—— —— —— (1949), Notes on the Theory of Aggression. *The Psychoanalytic Study of the Child*, 3/4:9-36. New York: International Universities Press.

ISAKOWER, O. (1938), A Contribution to the Patho-Psychology of Phenomena Associated with Falling Asleep. *Int. J. Psycho-Anal.*, 19:331-345.

—— (1939), On the Exceptional Position of the Auditory Sphere. *Int. J. Psycho-Anal.*, 20:340-348.

JACOBSON, E. (1954), The Self and the Object World: Vicissitudes of Their Infantile Cathexes and Their Influence on Ideational and Affective Development. *The Psychoanalytic Study of the Child*, 9:75-127. New York: International Universities Press.

[183]

BIBLIOGRAPHY

KATAN, M. (1954), The Importance of the Non-psychotic Part of the Personality in Schizophrenia. *Int. J. Psycho-Anal.*, 35:119-128.

KRIS, E. (1934), The Psychology of Caricature. *Psychoanalytic Explorations in Art.* New York: International Universities Press, 1952, pp. 173-188.

—— (1939), On Inspiration. *Psychoanalytic Explorations in Art.* New York: International Universities Press, 1952, pp. 291-302.

—— (1947), The Nature of Psychoanalytic Propositions and Their Validation. In: *Freedom and Experience,* ed. S. Hook & M. R. Konwitz. Ithaca, N.Y.: Cornell University Press.

—— (1950a), On Preconscious Mental Processes. *Psychoanalytic Explorations in Art.* New York: International Universities Press, 1952, pp. 303-318.

—— (1950b), Notes on the Development and on Some Current Problems of Psychoanalytic Child Psychology. *The Psychoanalytic Study of the Child,* 5:24-46. New York: International Universities Press.

—— (1950c), Introduction and Notes to *The Origins of Psychoanalysis: Letters to Wilhelm Fliess, Drafts and Notes: 1887-1902.* New York: Basic Books, 1954.

—— (1951), Ego Psychology and Interpretation in Psychoanalytic Therapy. *Psychoanal. Quart.,* 20:15-30.

—— & KAPLAN, A. (1952), Aesthetic Ambiguity. *Psychoanalytic Explorations in Art.* New York: International Universities Press, 1952, pp. 243-264.

KUBIE, L. S. (1958), *Neurotic Distortion of the Creative Processes.* Lawrence, Kansas: University of Kansas Press.

LEWIN, B. D. (1950), *The Psychoanalysis of Elation.* New York: Norton.

—— (1952), Phobic Symptoms and Dream Interpretation. *Psychoanal. Quart.,* 21:295-322.

LOEWENSTEIN, R. M. (1951), The Problem of Interpretation. *Psychoanal. Quart.,* 20:1-14.

—— (1958), Contribution to the Panel: Psychoanalytic Theory of Thinking, reported by J. A. Arlow, *J. Amer. Psychoanal. Assn.,* 6:143-153.

MARMOR, J. (1953), Orality in the Hysterical Personality. *J. Amer. Psychoanal. Assn.,* 1:656-671.

MODELL, A. H. (1958), The Theoretical Implications of Hallucinatory Experiences in Schizophrenia. *J. Amer. Psychoanal. Assn.,* 6:442-480.

NUNBERG, H. (1947), *Problems of Bisexuality as Reflected in Circumcision.* New York: International Universities Press, 1960.

[184]

BIBLIOGRAPHY

PIAGET, J. (1937), *The Construction of Reality in the Child.* New York: Basic Books, 1954.

RADO, S. (1939), Developments in the Psychoanalytic Conception and Treatment of the Neuroses. *Psychoanal. Quart.,* 8:427-437.

RANGELL, L. (1959), The Nature of Conversion. *J. Amer. Psychoanal. Assn.,* 7:632-662.

REICH, W. (1945), *Character Analysis.* New York: Orgone Institute Press.

RICHARDSON, G. A. & MOORE, R. A. (1963), On the Manifest Dream in Schizophrenia. *J. Amer. Psychoanal. Assn.,* 11:281-302.

RÓHEIM, G. (1955), *Magic and Schizophrenia.* New York: International Universities Press.

SCHILDER, P. (1928), *Introduction to a Psychoanalytic Psychiatry.* New York: International Universities Press, 1951.

SCHMIDEBERG, W. (1951) Agoraphobia as a Manifestation of Schizophrenia: The Analysis of a Case. *Psychoanal. Rev.,* 38:343-352.

SEARLES, H. F. (1962), The Differentiation between Concrete and Metaphorical Thinking in the Recovering Schizophrenic Patient. *J. Amer. Psychoanal. Assn.,* 10:22-49.

SPITZ, R. A. (1945), Hospitalism: An Inquiry into the Genesis of Psychiatric Conditions in Early Childhood. *The Psychoanalytic Study of the Child,* 1:53-74. New York: International Universities Press.

STERBA, R. (1934), The Fate of the Ego in Analytic Therapy. *Int. J. Psycho-Anal.,* 15:117-126.

WAELDER, R. (1930), The Principle of Multiple Function. *Psychoanal. Quart.,* 5:45-62, 1936.

—— (1951), The Structure of Paranoid Ideas. *Int. J. Psycho-Anal.,* 32:167-177.

—— (1963), Psychic Determinism and the Possibility of Predictions. *Psychoanal. Quart.,* 32:15-42.

WANGH, M. (1959), Structural Determinants of Phobia. *J. Amer. Psychoanal. Assn.,* 7:675-695.

WEISSMAN, P. (1954), Ego and Superego in Obsessional Character and Neurosis. *Psychoanal. Quart.,* 23:529-543.

WEXLER, M., (1951), The Structural Problem in Schizophrenia: Therapeutic Implications. *Int. J. Psycho-Anal.,* 32:157-166.

[185]

Index

[187]

Creativity *(cont'd)*
  and regression, 78
  see also Art, Artistic creation,
    Artistic experience
Cs., 21-23, 39
  and attention cathexis, 21
  and sleep, 116
  functions of, 21-22
  see also Pcs.

Daly, C. D., 69
Danger situation, 37; *see also*
  Anxiety
Daydreams
  and dreams, 128
  and regression, 73
Decathexis, 154, 159, 161, 162, 166,
    169
  and psychosis, 147
  and repression, 152
  and sleep, 116, 130
  of object representation, 157
  of object representation of *Ucs.,*
    151-153
  see also Psychosis, Regression
Defense, 38, 39
  and break with reality, 157-158
  and conflict, 112
  and countercathexis, 110
  and dream, 133, 135, 141, 143
  and hypochondriasis, 173, 174
  and megalomania, 170-171
  and psychosis, 144, 156-158, 171,
    175, 176
  and structural theory, 44
  and symptom formation, 174
  and theory of technique, 53-54,
    109-110
  and topographic theory, 44
  during sleep, 125-127
  neurotic versus psychotic, 159

unconscious nature of, 26-28, 53
  see also Anti-instinctual forces,
    Conflict, Denial, Displace-
    ment, Identification, Isolation,
    Projection, Reaction forma-
    tion, Repression, Substitution,
    Undoing
Defusion, 40
Deinstinctualization, 38, 93-94
Déjà vu, 78-79, 99
Delusion, 150, 174-177
  and aggression, 169
  and fantasy, 175
  and integrative function, 176
  and recathexis, 153
  and regression, 66
  and restitutive phase, 153
  and sadism, 169
  and structural theory, 169, 174-
    177
  messianic, 168-169
  of being observed, 66-67
  of world destruction, 146-147,
    166-168
Dement, W. C., 120
Dementia, 146
Denial, 38, 109
  and consciousness, 113
  in fantasy, 171
  see also Defense
Depersonalization, 79, 147
Depression
  and regression, 64
  oral wishes in, 64
  superego in, 40
Derealization, 79, 147
Desexualization, *see* Neutralization
Determinism, 7, 49
Developmental psychology, 76
Displacement, 86
  and mobility of cathexis, 90
  and primary process, 86